THE SECRETS OF TOP STUDENTS

TIPS, TOOLS, AND TECHNIQUES FOR ACING HIGH SCHOOL AND COLLEGE

STEFANIE WEISMAN

Valedictorian, Stuyvesant High School, and Albert Asher Green recipient
for highest GPA, Columbia University

Published by Sourcebooks, Inc.
P.O. Box 4410, Naperville, Illinois 60567-4410
(630) 961-3900
Fax: (630) 961-2168
www.sourcebooks.com

Library of Congress Cataloging-in-Publication Data

Weisman, Stefanie, author.
  The secrets of top students : tips, tools, and techniques for acing high school
and college / Stefanie Weisman, MA
     pages cm
 1. Study skills. 2. Test-taking skills. 3. Academic achievement. I. Title.
 LB1049.W445 2013
 371.30281—dc23

                         2012046675

     Printed and bound in the United States of America.
        VP 10 9 8 7

To my parents, Rhona and Bill. I could never have done it without you.
And to Bobby, for believing in me.

Contents

Introduction

Who Am I?

June 24, 1999. I am standing on the stage of Avery Fisher Hall in New York City, and I feel like I'm about to throw up. My hands are trembling, my stomach is turning, and my heart is pounding so violently that I can hear the blood rushing in my ears. I'm here to give my valedictory speech to the graduating class of Stuyvesant High School, one of the most competitive and academically rigorous schools in the country. The school is so big (more than 700 students in my class alone) that we had to rent out part of Lincoln Center to accommodate everyone.

The eyes of all my classmates and their parents follow me expectantly as I stride up to the podium with long, quick steps, trying to appear confident. Smoothing out the damp paper I have been crumpling in my hands, I begin to read in a quavering voice:

> The day I found out I was valedictorian was one of the happiest days of my life. But then, after the euphoria wore off, I realized something that sent a shiver down my spine: I had to make *a speech*. I'm a pretty shy person, and to stand here in front of thousands of people is not easy for

me. The terror I felt at public speaking almost made me wish my GPA was a few points lower, so I could avoid this nerve-racking ordeal. *Almost.* All I could do was write the best speech I could and try to present it without fainting. So now, I'm going to take a few deep breaths, hope for the best...and picture all of you in your underwear.

Okay, so maybe it wasn't the classiest speech in the world. But the crowd laughed, and I loosened up after that. I began to enjoy myself. It felt good to be the center of attention and to have people acknowledge all the hard work I had done over the past four years.

I never expected to become valedictorian of Stuyvesant, a public high school in New York City where fewer than 4 percent of students who take the entrance exam actually get in.[1] But my academic success didn't end there. Four years later, I again graduated with the highest GPA in my class—this time from Columbia College, the undergraduate school of Columbia University.[2] My grade point average was over a 4.0, causing lots of people to ask me how I got more than a "perfect" A. Simple, I told them: teachers at Columbia give out A+s, and each of those little beauties is worth 4.33!

I also came away with awards such as best senior thesis on a non-U.S. topic, best performance in Columbia's core curriculum—a required program for all undergrads that includes classes in literature, philosophy, music, art, language, science, and more—as well as summa cum laude and Phi Beta Kappa. Several years later I was admitted to Yale Law School, consistently ranked by *U.S.News & World Report* as the top law school in the country.[3] (I eventually decided not to go to law school, but that's a story for another book!)

Instead, I got a fellowship to attend New York University's Institute of Fine Arts, where I earned my Master's in Art History in a year and a half instead of the usual two and graduated with a GPA of 3.95. Around this time, I became interested in technology and went back to Columbia to get a second bachelor's degree, a BS in computer science. For two years I took nothing but courses in my new major. They were the hardest and most frustrating classes I had ever taken in my life, but I still managed to graduate magna cum laude, with a GPA of over 3.8.

As you can see, I've been a top student for a long time in a variety of areas. But it wasn't because I was so smart that everything came naturally to me. In fact, it was just the opposite: I had an undiagnosed learning disability that made it very hard for me to understand spoken words. I can't tell you how many times I would walk out of a classroom feeling like the teacher had been speaking a foreign language—and this was *not* in Spanish class.

In science labs, I would stare helplessly at the Bunsen burners and microscopes in front of me because I couldn't process verbal instructions. Most of my classmates, on the other hand, would merrily proceed to burn their organic compounds and gawk at the bacteria in their swamp water. I often felt frustrated and stupid, and there were times when I hated going to school.

But, ironically, I believe that my learning disability made me a better student. It meant that I had to become extra good at things like taking notes, studying, and writing papers—the big three in the life of a student—to compensate for my poor listening comprehension. I also became an expert at keeping myself motivated. I refused to let my learning difficulty limit what I could do. By the end of my academic career, I had developed an extensive collection of techniques, habits, and ways of thinking that helped me excel in school—and which I will now share with you!

However, I wanted this book to be based on more than just my experience. That's why I surveyed forty-five other academic superstars, including Rhodes scholars, high school and college valedictorians, students who made it into Yale Law School and Stanford Medical School, Intel Science Fair finalists, a winner of the Scripps

National Spelling Bee, and many more. If there's one thing I learned from this survey, it's that there is no one single way to achieve academic success.

Anyone who tells you that he or she knows the "correct" way to study either is lying or has a superiority complex. In fact, one of the keys to being a top student is recognizing how *you* learn best. Another is being able to adapt to each particular situation. This book will provide recommendations, advice, and ideas for improving your academic performance, but not hard and fast rules. Above all, it will help you discover the methods that work best for *you*.

Who Is This Book For?

This book is for anyone who wants to be a better student in high school or college—and by that I mean improving your GPA, studying more efficiently, honing your writing and critical thinking skills, and learning how to navigate the labyrinthine world of academia. All that's required are an open mind and a desire to excel. Whether you're at the bottom of the class, in the middle, or nearing the top and trying to take it to the next level, this book can help you.

By the way, you should *not* buy this book to become valedictorian. If that happens, great, but you'll go crazy if you put that kind of pressure on yourself because too many factors are beyond your control. I never aimed for the number-one spot in high school and college, but I got lucky—very, very lucky. This book will help you achieve your personal academic best, whatever that may be.

What Makes This Book Different from Other Study Aids?

First of all, if you're in a bookstore or library, look around you. Do you see any other books on how to improve your grades? Probably not. You will, however, notice lots of thick, brightly colored tomes on how to raise your score on the SAT and other standardized tests.

While there are shelves upon shelves of books on test prep, precious few address how to achieve academic success. But isn't doing well in school—which represents years of hard work to acquire knowledge and skills that will last you the rest of your life—more important than gaining a few points on a single exam?

That's a rhetorical question, by the way. Colleges, graduate schools, and employers care more about your grades and the rigor of your curriculum than they do about your standardized test scores. The truth is, most people want a quick fix. They figure that a good SAT, GRE, LSAT, or MCAT score will outweigh a poor or mediocre performance in school, but that just isn't the case. I'm not saying that standardized test scores don't matter; it's just that what you do in the classroom is so much more important.

> "A good GPA, even from a lousy high school, is a far better predictor of whether a student will finish college than a high mark on the SATs. Not coincidentally, GPAs reward perseverance, character, time-management skills, and the ability to work well with others."
>
> —Belinda Luscombe, "Failure Is Not a Bad Option: Resilience Helps Kids More Than High SATs Do," *Time* magazine, September 2012.

A small number of books do claim to show you how to get better grades. So what makes my book different and, dare I say, better? Here are some reasons.

- **My experience as the number-one student in both high school and college.** Most of the other writers have observed top students but have little firsthand experience. A few of them may have been *good* students in their time, but not *great* ones.

And wouldn't you rather get your advice from an actual top student than from someone who just writes about them?

- **My broad background in science and math, as well as the humanities**—unlike most of the other writers, who specialized in the latter and are somewhat clueless about the former. And let me tell you, the keys to success in STEM (science, technology, engineering, and math) are very different from those for the humanities. That's why I include sections on how to survive STEM, how to ace homework and tests in these subjects, and more.

- **My familiarity with today's technology.** I received my latest degree in 2011, while a lot of other writers sound as if they haven't been a student since 1967. Ever hear of the Internet, anyone? Technology can be both a help and a hazard to students, and it receives special attention in my book.

- **Advice and input from other outstanding students.** I've surveyed forty-five people with exceptional academic records on how they achieved success. Nearly half are Rhodes scholars, valedictorians, or salutatorians. Many are currently attending the nation's best law and medical schools. This group includes Rebecca Sealfon, the 1997 Scripps National Spelling Bee winner who made headlines with her extremely enthusiastic spelling of the final word "euonym"; and Justine Schluntz, Rhodes Scholar and 2010 NCAA Woman of the Year. Other participants include a winner of the Google Anita Borg Memorial Scholarship, Fulbright and Goldwater scholars, ESPN Academic All-American athlete-scholars, and Intel Science Fair finalists. The results of this survey and advice from the students themselves—indicated by "Survey Says" and "In Their Own Words"—provide unique insight into what it takes to succeed in school.

- **A holistic view of academic excellence.** Most guides fail to realize that there's a lot more to great grades than following cut-and-dried techniques for studying, writing papers, and taking tests. It requires the cultivation of your body, heart, and mind, much as you would expect of a top athlete. It's a lifestyle, not a set of instructions. You've got to eat well, sleep right, work hard, and, above all, have the drive and determination to succeed. That's why this book includes sections on things like the mind-body connection, improving your work ethic, and getting and staying motivated. I also discuss how to incorporate the findings from the latest research on education and learning into your everyday study habits.

- **No sugarcoating.** I won't do that, unlike many other study aid writers. No matter how many techniques you learn and how much you prepare, some things are out of your control. You can't always avoid taking classes you hate, having terrible teachers, or getting an unfair grade. The trick is knowing what to do when these bad things happen.

- **Information that works for high schoolers and college students.** Unlike most study aids, which are geared toward either one group or the other, this guide is meant for both. In high school, you should be learning skills that are transferable to college. If you're in college now, it's not too late to learn good study skills or improve on the ones you already have. Plus, a lot of high schools these days are just as hard as college, if not harder. I can tell you that after going to Stuyvesant High School, Columbia was practically a breeze!

Why Should You Want to Be a Better Student, Anyway?

If you're reading this book, chances are you already want to improve your academic performance (unless your parents have forced it on you—sorry, guys). But it couldn't hurt to remind you why grades are so important.

Reason 1: Competition for Scarce Resources

Every year, it gets harder to secure a place at a top university. Just look at these statistics from the February 5, 2011 edition of the *Wall Street Journal*:[4]

Number of freshman applications at UC Berkeley in fall 2001: 35,473

Number of freshman applications at UC Berkeley in fall 2011: 52,900

Admission rate for applicants to Yale, class of 2001: 17.8 percent

Admission rate for applicants to Yale, class of 2014: 7.5 percent

Scary, huh? Colleges and grad schools are becoming increasingly selective because they have to be—there are simply too many qualified applicants and not enough spots. The same is true of employment in this country. As the economy gets squeezed, competition for jobs skyrockets. And in these times of economic uncertainty, how you do in school is more important than ever.

Am I saying that getting great grades will guarantee you a spot in your dream school, or that you can't have a successful career without being a top student? No, of course not. But doing well in school does make it easier and more likely that you'll achieve these things.

Reason 2: It's Your Patriotic Duty

Seriously. Kind of. U.S. students are falling behind their counterparts in many (mostly Asian) countries, and this has an impact on America's standing in the global economy. You are competing not just with students in the same classroom, school, and nation, but with your peers all over the world. Consider President Obama's speech to U.S. students on the first day of school in 2009:

What you make of your education will decide nothing less than the future of this country. What you're learning in school today will determine whether we as a nation can meet our greatest challenges in the future....

Whatever you resolve to do, I want you to commit to it. I want you to really work at it. I know that sometimes, you get the sense from TV that you can be rich and successful without any hard work—that your ticket to success is through rapping or basketball or being a reality TV star, when chances are, you're not going to be any of those things. But the truth is, being successful is hard. You won't love every subject you study. You won't click with every teacher. Not every homework assignment will seem completely relevant to your life right this minute. And you won't necessarily succeed at everything the first time you try.[5]

And his 2011 State of the Union address, in which he said that the United States is facing a new "Sputnik moment":

We know what it takes to compete for the jobs and industries of our time. We need to out-innovate, out-educate, and out-build the rest of the world....

We need to teach our kids that it's not just the winner of the Super Bowl who deserves to be celebrated, but the winner of the science fair. We need to teach them that success is not a function of fame or PR, but of hard work and discipline.[6]

I know it might be difficult to think of your academic success as being for the greater good. Some of you may feel inspired by the President's words, others apathetic. But whatever the case, doing well in school will benefit both you and the nation. It's a win-win situation!

Reason 3: The Sense of Satisfaction and Accomplishment

It's a great feeling when you accomplish something through hard work and effort—when you can pat yourself on the back and say, "Job well done." Whether you raised your GPA a few points, finally got an A on your pre-calculus test, mastered the Spanish subjunctive, or wrote a stellar paper on the legacy of Socrates in Western civilization, you can be proud of having done your best.

Reason 4: The Quest for Knowledge

That's right, people actually go to school to learn! In general, the better a student you are, the stronger your critical thinking skills will be and the more you'll know about the world around you. When you write a paper, you're learning how to synthesize new ideas from diverse types of information; when you study for a test, you're figuring out how to apply the concepts you were taught in class; when you memorize facts and figures, you're adding to your knowledge base and your ability to put things in context.

And, in the end, this is the real reason for going to school—to become an educated, knowledgeable, rational human being, not to get straight As or go to an Ivy League college or even to get a high-paying job (though these things are nice too!).

Okay, enough with my little spiel. It's time to get down to business.

CHAPTER 1
What's My Motivation?

MOTIVATION IS ONE OF the toughest and most nebulous aspects of becoming a better student, yet it's also one of the most essential. The human mind is a complicated thing, and there aren't any step-by-step instructions you can follow to give yourself an attitude adjustment. But knowing what's at stake, what motivates others to succeed, and what your goals are is a pretty good start. And since you're reading this book, chances are you already have an interest in doing better in school—and that's half the battle!

In high school and college, one way I stayed motivated was by thinking of myself as a top athlete. I got up early to train (study and do homework), took my workouts (classes) seriously, prepared for the upcoming meet (the exam) every day, and maintained healthy sleep and eating habits (this one's straightforward). I took pride in my work and my achievements. For me, becoming valedictorian of Stuyvesant was *kind of* like winning the Olympics.

In general, though, students don't get as much attention as athletes. They don't have crowds of people shouting their name, or fans following their every move, or lucrative product endorsements. That's why, to do well in academics, you have to know what you're studying for. You can't always depend on other people to cheer you on, so you've got to have something deep inside yourself that keeps you going. This chapter will look at how you can get—and stay—motivated from orientation all the way to graduation.

How Important Are Grades, Anyway?

Let's take a look at the most common reason for wanting a better GPA: it improves your chances of getting into a good school and landing a good job. This may sound obvious to many of you, but it's worth taking a closer look at why grades matter. *The more you understand about what you're working for, the easier it is to stay motivated.*

When applying to college and grad school, you're asked to provide such a wide range of information—your transcript, standardized test scores, essays, letters of recommendation, extracurriculars, work experience, and so on—that it's hard to know how much your academic performance really matters. Well, I'm here to tell you that it's one of the most important parts of your application.

I'm not saying that you have no chance of getting into your dream school with a mediocre transcript, or that a high grade point average will guarantee you a seat at Harvard. But admissions officers place more emphasis on your grades—especially the ones from rigorous, high-level classes—than almost any other factor. Yes, schools like to see that you're well rounded, but that doesn't mean it's okay to neglect your GPA. Plus, if your standardized test scores are high but your grades are low, schools may start to wonder whether you've really been applying yourself for the past four years.

Every year, college admissions officers from around the country take a survey on what really matters to them. In 2010, grades in college prep courses, strength of the student's course of study, and grades in all courses, in that order, were three of the top four factors. College prep courses, by the way, include Advanced Placement (AP) and International Baccalaureate (IB) courses, college courses taken while in high school, and other advanced or college-level coursework.

Grades in these classes were the highest ranked factor, with

86.5 percent of respondents giving grades a rating of "considerable importance." Next came strength of curriculum at 70.7 percent, admission test scores at 57.8 percent, and grades in all courses at 45.6 percent. The following table from the NACAC (National Association for College Admission Counseling) gives you a good idea of how colleges really view your application:

How Colleges View a Student's Application		
Factor	Considerable Importance	Moderate Importance
Grades in college prep courses	86.5%	11.5%
Strength of applicant's curriculum	70.7%	22.0%
Admission test scores (SAT, ACT)	57.8%	32.0%
Grades in all courses	45.6%	43.9%
Essay or writing sample	26.4%	37.5%
Teacher recommendation	17.4%	47.7%
Student's demonstrated interest in the school	20.7%	27.0%
Counselor recommendation	17.1%	50.0%

(continues)

How Colleges View a Student's Application, cont.		
Factor	**Considerable Importance**	**Moderate Importance**
Class rank	16.3%	42.2%
Interview	6.6%	26.3%
Subject test scores (AP, IB)	7.0%	27.2%
Extracurricular activities	8.9%	43.9%
SAT II Scores	5.0%	11.0%
Work	1.7%	20.2%

Source: Melissa Clinedinst and David Hawkins, "2010 State of College Admission," National Association for College Admission Counseling, accessed December 12, 2012, http://www.nacacnet .org/research/PublicationsResources/Marketplace/Documents/SoCA2010.pdf.

The fact that grades in college-prep courses were the highest ranked factor begs the question: **how many advanced classes should you take while in high school?** The (frustratingly vague) answer is: the highest number you can manage without significantly lowering your GPA. This is different for every person, and there's no number that will guarantee admission to your dream school. It also depends on how many advanced classes your school offers, what your interests are, and what colleges you want to attend. Don't make yourself crazy by filling your entire schedule with AP classes; your curriculum should be challenging without being overwhelming. It's a good idea to contact the schools you're interested in attending to get a sense of their expectations.

If you're trying to get into a highly selective school, your transcript should be top-notch. According to the admissions FAQs on Harvard's website, for example, "the strongest applicants take the most rigorous secondary school curricula available to them," with most admitted students "rank[ing] in the top 10–15 percent of their graduating classes."[7]

Similarly, Yale states that the high school transcript is the "single most important document" in a student's application, and while your academic record can make up for a lackluster SAT or ACT score, "it is unlikely that high standardized test scores will persuade the admissions committee to disregard an undistinguished secondary-school record."[8]

Many of the highest ranked colleges have stopped releasing the average high-school GPA of accepted students, but of those that do, Princeton reports a 3.9, the University of Pennsylvania a 3.8, Vanderbilt University a 3.7, and the University of California at Berkeley a 4.0.[9] The expectations of many good but less competitive schools are also startlingly high. Take a look at the average high-school GPA of students accepted by these "more selective" schools (a step down from "most selective"). The numbers speak for themselves:

Average High-School GPA for More Selective Colleges	
School	**Average High-School GPA**
Binghamton University-SUNY	3.6
George Washington University (DC)	3.6
Pepperdine University (CA)	3.7

(continues)

Average High-School GPA for More Selective Colleges, cont.	
School	**Average High-School GPA**
University of the Pacific (CA)	3.5
Rensselaer Polytechnic Institute (NY)	3.7
Fordham University (NY)	3.5
University of Georgia	3.8
Hofstra University (NY)	3.4
University of Delaware	3.5

Source: Anne McGrath, ed., U.S.News & World Report Ultimate College Guide 2011, Table: More Selective Schools, p. 96. Naperville, IL: Sourcebooks, Inc.

Once you've made it into college, don't expect to be able to coast for the next four years. If you're thinking of going to grad school—whether to a master's or PhD program, law school, medical school, or business school—it's more important than ever to keep your grades up. Here's a chilling fact: as of 2012, the median GPA of students entering Yale Law School was 3.90, with 75 percent having 3.98 or higher.

Now, Yale Law School is one of the hardest schools to get into in the country, so you shouldn't take its standards as, well, standard. But most competitive graduate programs expect a GPA of 3.5 or higher, especially in the area you're going to specialize in. The specific requirements for different types of grad schools are too numerous to include in this book, but you should keep in mind that the higher your college GPA, the better your chances of getting merit-based financial aid.

Okay, so getting better grades will help you get into more prestigious institutions, but **does it really matter where you go to school?** Well, that question opens up a huge can of worms. People have asked for a long time whether students learn better in more selective schools. According to recent research, the answer is a qualified yes.

In their study "Improving Undergraduate Learning: Findings and Policy Recommendations from the SSRC-CLA Longitudinal Project," Richard Arum, Josipa Roksa, and Esther Cho found that the following types of students were more likely to improve on the Collegiate Learning Assessment (CLA) test—which measures critical thinking, complex reasoning, and written communication skills—at the end of four years:[10]

- Students who spent more hours studying alone.
- Students who took courses requiring both significant reading (more than forty pages per week) and writing (more than twenty pages over the course of the semester).
- Students who said that their school's faculty had high expectations.
- Students who had done more advanced coursework in high school.

Although all institutions had some students who showed substantial improvement on the CLA, the schools that are more selective had more of them. According to the research, a school's selectivity does "make a difference in improving student performance," with "23 percent of variation in CLA performance occur[ring] across institutions."[11] *Hard-to-get-into schools are more likely to have rigorous classes, students with advanced backgrounds, and faculty with high expectations.* For example, 71 percent of students at highly selective institutions had twenty or more pages of writing in at least one course per semester, compared to only 39 percent of students in less selective schools.[12] Arum and Roksa define highly selective colleges as those with "students at the 25th percentile having combined verbal and math SAT scores higher than 1,150" and less selective colleges as those with "students at the 25th percentile having combined scores lower than 950."[13]

In their book *Academically Adrift: Limited Learning on College Campuses*, Arum and Roksa mention another reason why top schools foster greater learning:

> Being surrounded by peers who are well prepared for college-level work is likely to shape the climate of the institution as well as specific student experiences. Having high-performing students in the classroom can help improve achievement of all students, including those who have accumulated fewer skills before entering college.[14]

At Columbia, I definitely felt challenged by my professors, my classmates, and my course requirements, and while those high expectations could be annoying or even overwhelming at times, they pushed me to learn much more than I would have otherwise.

Of course, school is about more than learning for learning's sake. It's also about gaining the skills and experience necessary for a successful (and hopefully lucrative) career. Doing well in school will give you an edge when you enter the job market. More than 73 percent of employers screen candidates based on GPA, according to the National Association of Colleges and Employers' Job Outlook 2012 survey. Most use 3.0 as their cutoff, but some companies set the bar much higher.[15]

In addition, 73 percent of employers look for a strong work ethic in a candidate's resumé, and having top marks goes a long way toward showing you're a hard worker. Grades are especially important for someone who's just graduating and doesn't have a lot of work experience. What's more, having significant academic awards can really make your resumé stand out from the crowd.

The school you attend may also have an impact on *your future salary*. Take a look at the 2012–2013 starting median salaries and mid-career salaries of a sampling of "most selective," "more selective," and "less selective" schools, as provided by www.payscale.com.

Median Salaries for Different Types of Colleges		
School	**Starting Median Salary**	**Mid-Career Median Salary**
Most Selective		
Harvard	$50,700	$111,000
Stanford	$58,200	$114,000
Yale	$48,900	$105,000
Columbia	$54,700	$105,000
Princeton	$58,300	$137,000
Brown	$52,400	$109,000
MIT	$68,400	$118,000
More Selective		
Binghamton University	$49,100	$84,600
George Washington University	$47,300	$93,100
SUNY—Stony Brook	$45,800	$91,000
Northeastern University	$50,400	$84,900
Pepperdine University	$44,700	$88,900
University of Florida	$46,200	$80,800
University of Maryland	$49,100	$87,100

(continues)

Median Salaries for Different Types of Colleges, cont.		
School	**Starting Median Salary**	**Mid-Career Median Salary**
Less Selective		
Syracuse University	$47,000	$86,200
Florida State University	$39,000	$73,400
University of Nebraska	$39,000	$72,600
Clark University	$39,600	$78,500
University of South Carolina	$40,500	$71,500
University of Cincinnati	$44,800	$76,600
University of Denver	$44,500	$82,000

Source: 2012–2013 PayScale College Salary Report, www.payscale.com/college-salary-report-2013 /full-list-of-schools.

As you can see, the alumni of more selective schools tend to have bigger salaries, both when they graduate and when they're midway through their careers. The median beginning salary for Ivy League grads is 32 percent higher than that of the alumni of small, private liberal-arts colleges, according to a 2008 *Wall Street Journal* article.[16] However, this isn't the whole story. The difference in pay may be due more to the types of jobs their alumni pursue than to how selective the school is. A large percentage of Ivy Leaguers are drawn to high-paying jobs in finance. And the graduates of many engineering schools have higher median salaries than the alums of more selective colleges. If you want to know which colleges give you the biggest bang for your buck in terms of initial cost and alumni salaries, take a look at PayScale's 2012 ROI Rankings: College Education Value Compared, at www.payscale .com/college-education-value.

No matter what school you attend, however, ambition and hard work can help you get a higher salary. Researchers Alan Krueger and Stacy Dale have made the intriguing discovery that "[s]tudents who attended more selective colleges do not earn more than other students who were accepted and rejected by comparable schools but attended less selective colleges."[17] In other words, people who applied to top-tier schools but did not go—*regardless of whether they were accepted*—wound up earning salaries on par with alumni from those schools.

This could be because students who are ambitious enough to apply to selective schools are likely to pursue high-paying jobs, no matter where they graduate from. Studying more in college is also associated with higher wages, according to researchers Philip Babcock and Mindy Marks. Of the individuals they surveyed, "a standard deviation in hours studied…is associated with a wage gain of 8.8 percent."[18] So it seems that working hard and doing well in school can give your salary a boost.

The bottom line is that no school is right for everyone. It depends on you and your priorities, and many people are perfectly happy outside the ivory tower. But research supports that a more selective institution can help you learn, and having a strong academic record can help you succeed in the workplace.

You've Gotta Have Goals

If you're in high school, do you know where you want to go to college? If you're an undergrad, do you have your sights set on a specific career or grad school? More importantly, do you know *how* to achieve these things? Getting detailed about your dreams can make a huge difference in your performance. Students who wrote about their goals and planned how to achieve them raised their GPA by 30 percent, according to a 2010 study at the University of Toronto. These students also reported feeling less anxious and stressed.[19]

The key is to *break your goals down into manageable chunks*. If your aim is simply, "Get into a top-tier college," that's not going to help you much. If, instead, you deconstruct this into highly specific sub-goals—such as (1) get my math grade up this term, (2) take a practice SAT exam once a week, (3) find a teacher who can write my letter of recommendation, and (4) join the school band—you'll find it much easier to stay on track. To help you get started, I've included some goal-writing exercises at the end of this chapter.

It's a good idea to research schools and careers you're interested in as soon as possible—preferably years in advance—so you can develop concrete goals. If you're in high school, make a list of colleges you would like to attend, including dream and safety schools. Find out the average GPA (or, if that's not available, class percentile) and standardized test scores of accepted students. If you're in college and plan on continuing your education, do the same thing for grad schools.

The Princeton Review and *U.S. News & World Report* (available online at www.usnews.com/education) provide rankings and admissions information for colleges and graduate programs, and are fantastic resources. Read up about the requirements for careers you're considering, and ask people in those industries for advice on how to prepare.

For a good (and free) introduction to many different types of careers, including their educational requirements, check out the U.S. Bureau of Labor Statistics' *Occupational Outlook Handbook*, available online at www.bls.gov/oco/ (click on the Index link to see a list of jobs). Knowing what's required will make it easier to set goals for your GPA, your curriculum, your test scores, your skill set, and much, much more—and with goals comes *motivation*.

If you don't know what you want to do with the rest of your life, however, don't despair. (I was in this situation throughout high school and college—which might explain why I went from history to art history to considering law school to computer science!) Many students are conflicted about their career paths, and this is the perfect time for exploration. Don't let uncertainty about your future overwhelm you! Keep yourself motivated by focusing on more immediate, short-term goals, such as:

- Completing the coursework in each class to the best of your ability.
- Fulfilling your school's graduation requirements.
- Preparing applications for college or graduate school.
- Applying for internships or jobs.
- Studying for standardized tests.

If you're in college, you have additional goals such as:

- Deciding on a major. You can do this by looking at the requirements for each department, taking a wide variety of classes to see which ones you like the best, researching what kind of jobs are available for the majors you're considering, and taking a career evaluation test at your school's career services center.
- Completing the requirements for your major, once you declare one.
- Deciding on and completing a senior thesis, if required.

Even if you don't have concrete plans for the future, try to do the best you can in every class. Good grades will help you no matter what you choose to pursue in the end. You'll learn valuable skills in almost every subject, and at the very least you'll come away with a better sense of what you like and don't like. *Remember: Don't let uncertainty about your future paralyze your present.*

What Motivates Top Students? (Hint: It's Not Just Grades)

It's tough to figure out what makes top students tick—but in an attempt to do this, I asked my group of scholars how much they attribute several factors to their academic success, on a scale of 1 to 10. Here are the results:

Factors Top Students Attribute to Their Success	
Factor	Average Importance
Determination	8.98
Hard Work	8.82
Desire to Learn	8.73
Pressure from Self	8.69
Ambition	8.64
Self-Control	8.22
Intelligence	8.02
Supportive Family	7.51
Good Teachers	7.04
Good Time Management	6.93
Parental Pressure	4.20
Peer Pressure	3.25

Let's take a closer look at these results.

- **Determination.** This was the top-scoring factor among high-achieving students, and it's a telling sign of their attitude toward school. For most of them, their primary motivation didn't come from external sources such as pushy parents and teachers or from being such geniuses that everything came naturally to them. It came from the inside—from their own desire to succeed. Force of will, combined with **good old-fashioned hard work** (which was the second most highly rated factor), helped them come out on top.

- **Desire to learn.** Most top students are in it for more than just the grades. They actually care about what they're learning. It's important to have curiosity about the world, a longing to understand things. Take me, for instance—I'm a voracious reader of all kinds of books, Wikipedia is my favorite website, and I feel bored and unhappy if I'm not constantly learning.

In Their Own Words

"Worry less about grades, more about learning the stuff. If you focus on learning the stuff, you'll get good grades, for the most part. If you focus on grades, you'll drive yourself nuts."

—Top student and graduate of Carnegie Mellon University

- **Pressure from self.** Like determination, this high-scoring factor reflects a student's inner desire to succeed. It was ranked much higher than external forces, such as pressure from parents and peers.
- **Ambition.** This was another high-scoring factor, and though it's similar to determination, ambition is more focused on the end result than the here and now. For many top students, getting high grades is important because it will help them pursue their careers and achieve personal goals.
- **Intelligence.** Okay, no one's saying intelligence doesn't matter, but it's considered significantly less important than things like determination and hard work. The point is, you don't have to be a genius to excel in school, and most top students have to work hard to get where they are.
- I'm going to combine the following factors here: **supportive family and parental pressure**. As you can see from the chart,

top students ranked having a supportive family much higher than having parents who constantly nagged them to get straight As. In my survey, the vast majority—75 percent—said that their parents were supportive. Only 18 percent said they felt pressured by their parents to get good grades, while 7 percent had parents who didn't care much at all about their school performance. This is important to note at a time when so-called "tiger mothers"—parents who aggressively push their children to excel in school—have been receiving a great deal of attention. Few of the high achievers in my survey had such domineering parents.

- **Good teachers.** The results indicate that having good teachers is important but not extremely critical to top students. Having teachers who can inspire you and push you to do your best is great, but you shouldn't depend on this being the case. You're probably going to have some truly awful teachers in your academic career—I know I did—so you should be prepared for all personality types.

- **Peer pressure.** This does not seem to be a critical factor. While it may help to have friends who challenge you to excel, most top students didn't feel this was vital to their success. Again, these external factors seem less important than the students' self-defined and self-determined desire to succeed.

In Their Own Words

Some students don't hit their stride until after high school. Consider what motivated these top college achievers.

"In college I was much more focused on getting top grades given my plan for going to medical school."

—College valedictorian, now a doctor

"In high school I was lazy and immature. I figured that if I was smarter than all of my classmates, why should I have to work as hard as them? As soon as I hit college I did a 180. It came down to working hard and realizing that it wasn't just about me. I was paying to go to classes, so I needed to go, simple as that."

—Student at Yale Law School

"I did not recognize my lack of personal academic accomplishment in high school until the college admission process. I was in the middle of the pack at a very competitive high school and, until filling out college applications, had not realized my desire to be better than 'middle of the pack.' The college process was definitely a blow to my ego, but it was the kick that I needed and am so grateful for today. When I arrived at college, I had a newfound desire to reach my potential. [T]hat combined with maturity of both self and study skills allowed me to be the type of student that I wanted to be throughout college."

—Student at NYU Law School

Motivation is something you have to keep working at your entire life. It doesn't happen overnight—it's a gradual, complicated, and deeply personal process. For most top students, something deep inside them compelled them to succeed. The way I see it, there are good and bad forms of motivation. The good kind comes from wanting to improve yourself and fulfill your potential, and consists of factors such as:

1.   The desire to learn.
2.   Taking pride in your work.
3.   Wanting to do the best you can.

4. Believing you can achieve great things through effort.
5. Setting high expectations for yourself.
6. Trying to achieve realistic goals for your future.

Bad motivation, on the other hand, should be avoided as much as possible, and includes:

1. Wanting to be better than everyone else.
2. Seeking praise from your parents and teachers.
3. Being afraid of failure.
4. Feeling guilty or worthless if a goal is not achieved.
5. Trying to achieve a very narrow goal with a low probability of success, such as becoming valedictorian or getting into Yale Law School.

This kind of motivation can be destructive because it puts undue stress on you, turns your classmates into The Enemy, gives you potentially unrealistic expectations, makes you afraid to take risks, and causes you to rely too much on others for support and encouragement. It's unrealistic to expect to eliminate all bad motivation from your life, but your resolve to improve your grades will be much stronger and healthier if you focus on the good kind.

Don't forget that your happiness is the most important thing, and that you should never equate your GPA or school with your sense of self-worth. This is a trap that many ambitious students fall into. If you're feeling overwhelmed, take a step back and remind yourself that **you are not your grades**. Don't be afraid to talk to someone about how you're feeling.

I must admit, I was guilty of employing some forms of bad motivation when I was a student, and I can tell you from experience that they'll only make you unhappy. It can be a struggle to cultivate good motivation and block out the bad, but you'll be much happier and more fulfilled in the end.

Do You Have to Be a Perfectionist to Be a Top Student?

When most people think of top students, they picture overly stressed, hyper-competitive kids who beat themselves up for anything less than an A. And while this stereotype may be true for some high achievers, being a perfectionist actually *decreases* your chances of academic success for a number of reasons. Focusing on perfection:

1. Makes it difficult to start a project because it may turn out less than perfect.
2. Makes it difficult to complete a project because it never seems good enough.
3. Makes it difficult to budget time, as the perfectionist doesn't want to move on to a new project until the first one is done right (which may be never).
4. Makes it difficult to learn from mistakes.
5. Makes the perfectionist less likely to take risks—for example, trying challenging projects or taking subjects that he or she feels "weak" in.
6. Makes the person more susceptible to low self-esteem, depression, and anxiety.

Studies show that being able to accept failure is critical for learning and may actually give your brain a boost. In a 2012 French experiment, students were given a set of difficult anagram problems which none of them could solve. One group was then told that experiencing difficulty is a normal part of learning, while the others were told that the researchers were looking at what strategies they used. When they were later given a test measuring working memory capacity, an important indicator of intelligence, the failure-is-normal group scored significantly better.

So why would a simple pep talk lead to higher scores? According to one of the researchers, Frederique Autin, "By being obsessed with success, students are afraid to fail, so they are reluctant to take difficult steps to master new material. Acknowledging that difficulty is a crucial part of learning could stop a vicious circle in which difficulty creates feelings of incompetence that in turn disrupts learning."[20] In other words, *realizing that it's okay to make mistakes can help you become a better student.*

Students also tend to do better when they're not overly concerned with looking smart. In a startling study, Claudia Mueller and Carol Dweck showed how a single sentence—"You must have worked hard at these problems," said to a group of fifth graders after they completed a test of nonverbal puzzles—led the students to choose more challenging practice problems, work harder at them, try to learn from their mistakes, and score 30 percent better on a test with a difficulty level similar to the first.[21]

By contrast, a group of kids who were told "You must be smart at these problems" went for the easier puzzles, gave up more easily, did not try to learn from their errors, and scored 20 percent worse on the follow-up test. Since they were told they were smart, they were more afraid to take risks and make mistakes that could hurt their fragile self-image; but in the end, this overly cautious strategy backfired on them.

In a separate study, Dweck also found that students who have a "growth mind-set"—that is, the belief that intelligence is malleable—had a steady increase in math grades over a period of two years, while those who believe that intelligence is fixed saw a drop in their grades.[22]

In Their Own Words

"Don't be afraid to admit that you don't understand something. Ask for help if you don't get it. That's how you learn!"

—Goldwater Scholar

The bottom line is that being a perfectionist is more likely to hurt than help you. As these experiments show, changing your attitude about how you learn can have a big impact on your performance. So what does this mean for you? Whether you're a perfectionist or not, pay close attention to how you react when things don't go your way.

Since you don't have a researcher telling you that failure is okay or praising you for your effort, you'll have to become your own encourager. When you find yourself having negative thoughts— "I'm not smart enough," "This subject's too hard for me," "I'm not good at [fill in the blank]"—stop for a moment and give yourself a talking-to. Remind yourself that:

- Intelligence is expandable, not fixed.
- Your brain is like a muscle; the more you use it, the stronger it gets.
- Mistakes are a natural part of learning. View them as an opportunity, not as something to be ashamed of.
- You can learn anything with time and effort.
- Most people who succeed do so through hard work, not inborn ability.

Famous sayings like "If at first you don't succeed, try, try again," and "Genius is 1 percent inspiration, 99 percent perspiration," are also good models to follow. When you succeed, take pride in the effort you put in, not your ability. It can be hard to have only yourself for encouragement, so partner up with some friends and support each other when the going gets rough, or ask a parent to egg you on. Just make sure they give you the right kind of encouragement.

Six Simple Ways to Stay Motivated

In addition to setting goals and adjusting your attitude, here are six easy ways to get psyched about school.

1. **Study something you like.** Although in high school you may have little control over your schedule, in college you'll be overwhelmed with choices. Make sure you major in something you like and if you go to graduate school, choose a program you're passionate about. This may sound obvious, but lots of people fail to follow this simple rule. They major in something because it sounds practical, and they go to law or medical or business school because they feel it's expected of them. (I almost fell into this trap.) Their motivation quickly fades as they spend countless hours studying something that just isn't them. (Not that there's anything *wrong* with law or medical or business school; it's just that you have to *want* to do it.)

In Their Own Words

"College allowed me to mostly focus on…those subjects I was really interested in…. I had more freedom."

—Top student, now an aerospace engineer

"In college I was able to focus my efforts on the few subjects that mattered most to me."

—Winner of Best in Category, Intel Science Fair

2. **Take things one day at a time.** If you're constantly thinking too far ahead—weeks, months, or even years into the future—you'll be overwhelmed by all the things you have to do. Of course you should be aware of when your projects are due, your test dates, your application deadlines, and so on, but you should also be able to push these things to the back of your mind and focus on the task at hand.

3. **Watch the game show *Jeopardy!*** Seriously! *Jeopardy!* exercises your brain, inspires you to learn, and puts you in an environment where knowledge is something valuable. It's a great feeling when you come across a question that none of the contestants can answer and realize, "Hey, I *know* that!" I don't recommend most of the other trivia shows on TV, though, because they emphasize pop culture and dumb luck more than the kind of stuff you learn in school.

4. **Reward yourself.** Have some concrete plans for how you're going to celebrate after a particularly grueling project or exam. Go out with friends, see a show, eat in a fancy restaurant, take a mini-vacation—whatever floats your boat.

5. **Get lots of sleep.** It's hard to stay motivated when you can barely keep your eyes open; being well-rested keeps your spirits high. More on this when we discuss the mind-body connection.

6. **Cast out negative thoughts.** One way to do this is by having a mantra—a short, positive, self-affirming statement that you say again and again and again and again. Whenever you feel like you're not good enough (and believe me, everyone thinks this at some point or another), repeat your mantra in your head—or out loud if you're by yourself. You can also write it out a few times a day for added reinforcement. It should be something simple and direct, like, "I am smart. I am special. I am strong. I can do whatever I set my mind to." Or, "I'm proud of myself for doing my best. That's all anyone can ask of me." You may be surprised by how a few simple phrases can change your whole outlook on life.

Exercises

Exercise 1:

This exercise is designed to make you think about your goals and how to achieve them. According to the 2010 University of Toronto study mentioned earlier, simply writing about your goals can improve academic performance. There are no right or wrong answers here, but try to be as specific as you can.*

Step 1: Using a separate piece of paper, spend about two minutes describing your goals for your education and future career. Just write whatever comes into your head—don't worry about how it sounds or if it's grammatically correct.

Step 2: Read over your answer to Step 1. Based on what you wrote, come up with a list of five specific goals. For each one, write down why it's important to you, three sub-goals necessary to accomplish it, and when you could realistically achieve it. This'll help you break down your goals into manageable chunks.

Goal 1: _____

_____

This is important to me because _____

_____

*If, after completing this exercise, you'd like additional guidance on setting your goals, consider the Self-Authoring Program available (for a fee) at www.selfauthoring.com, developed by the researchers responsible for the University of Toronto study.

Sub-goal 1: _____

_____

Sub-goal 2: _____

_____

Sub-goal 3: _____

_____

When would I realistically be able to achieve this goal? _____

_____

Goal 2: _____

_____

This is important to me because _____

_____

Sub-goal 1: _____

_____

Sub-goal 2: _____

_____

Sub-goal 3: _____

_____

When would I realistically be able to achieve this goal? _____

_____

Goal 3: _____

_____

This is important to me because _____

_____

Sub-goal 1: _____

_____

Sub-goal 2: _____

_____

Sub-goal 3: _____

_____

When would I realistically be able to achieve this goal? _____

_____

Goal 4: _____

_____

This is important to me because _____

_____

Sub-goal 1: _____

_____

Sub-goal 2: _____

_____

Sub-goal 3: _____

_____

When would I realistically be able to achieve this goal? _____

_____

Goal 5: _____

_____

This is important to me because _____

_____

Sub-goal 1: _____

_____

Sub-goal 2: _____

_____

Sub-goal 3: _____

_____

When would I realistically be able to achieve this goal? _____

_____

Exercise 2:

List five things you can do to reward yourself after successfully completing a task—for example, watching a movie, taking a bubble bath, or eating your favorite dessert. Having specific things to look forward to can be an excellent motivator.

1. _____

_____

2. _____

_____

3. _____

_____

4. _____

_____

5. _____

_____

Exercise 3:

Write down a mantra (a short, self-affirming statement). Try to say it—either out loud or in your head, whatever you feel more comfortable with—at least once a day, and whenever you have negative thoughts. This is an easy and effective way to increase motivation.

Tip: Your mantra shouldn't be an unrealistic or overly demanding statement such as "I am smarter than everyone else," or "I must get an A on this physics test." It should be something that reminds you of your good qualities and gives you confidence in yourself. For example, "I am proud of myself for doing my best. That's all anyone can ask of me."

_____

_____

_____

_____

Chapter 2
Time Management 101

Forget physics, forget organic chem, forget reading James Joyce's *Ulysses*—organizing your time is one of the biggest challenges you'll face in your academic career. What with classes, homework, extracurriculars, job, social life, family obligations, and fun, the schedule of a high school or college student could make even chess master Garry Kasparov's head spin. A good time manager will not only meet deadlines, but space things out to avoid cramming and rushing as much as humanly possible. How you organize your schedule is a highly personal thing, but there are some steps everyone can take to make the most of their time.

Taking Control of Your Time

Start by creating a semester calendar in which you write down events such as midterms, finals, regular tests, papers, presentations, vacations, and holidays. You can often fill in a lot of these dates at the beginning of the term when your teacher hands out the syllabus. Being able to see a whole month at a glance makes it easy to know when your crunch and catch-up times will be. Put the calendar on your wall as a constant reminder of *the big picture*.

You also need something to keep track of the nitty-gritty of your schedule. For day-to-day details, choose one of the following:

Survey Says

Good time management is very important to top students. In ranking factors that they attributed to their academic success, 23 percent gave good time management a perfect 10, 16 percent gave it a 9, and most gave it more than a 5. When asked to rate how organized they were, 39 percent gave themselves a 4 (out of 5), 16 percent gave themselves a 5, and 25 percent a 3.

day planner, basic notepad, Google Calendar, regular calendar, mobile app, or to-do list. It doesn't matter if it's simple or sophisticated, expensive or free, as long as you're comfortable with it and can keep everything in one place.

If you have multiple schedules, you're much more likely to miss something. Use your timekeeper of choice for school assignments as well as dates, meet-ups, parties, extracurriculars, jobs—pretty much your whole life!—and review it at least once a day to stay on top of things. Here are some tips on how to supercharge your schedule:

- If you make a to-do list, **include a deadline next to each task**. Cross out each item when it's done, and when most have a line through them, start a new list. I like to keep my list on the computer so I can move more pressing tasks to the top and put the extra-urgent ones in bold.
- If you use a planner or calendar, **give yourself a countdown for major events**. For something like a paper or an exam that is way off in the future, add reminders that it's coming up in one month, two weeks, one week, and so on.
- If you break up a complicated task (like writing a paper) into separate steps, **include a deadline for when each step should be completed**.
- **Set artificial deadlines**. Make major projects due a few days before their actual deadline so you'll have time to tie up loose ends. When you add these to your schedule, make sure you

include "A.D." (for artificial deadline) and "R.D." (for real deadline) to remember which is which.

- **Google Calendar** is pretty great (and free). All you need is a Gmail account and Internet access. You can include as many tasks and events as you want; view your schedule by day, week, or month; plan your schedule down to the hour; and color code for different classes. If you use it, though, always have a pad of paper to write down your tasks as they come up, and transfer them to your online calendar at least once a day.

A great way to stay on top of things is to *talk through what you have to do today, every morning, out loud to yourself.* Your one-sided conversation should go something like this: "Okay, I've got Intro to Physics followed by Spanish in the morning, then I've got a break from 12 to 1. It's nice out today, so I'll eat my lunch outside while I review my notes. Then I've got Econ, and that's right next to the gym so I can do a few laps afterward, and I told Jenny I would meet her for dinner in the cafeteria. Too bad it's meatloaf night. Then, let's see, I have those math problems due tomorrow, so I'll finish that when I get home, and I've got to start writing a draft of my paper on *To the Lighthouse.* Oh yeah, and before I go to sleep I can do a little studying for the Econ test I've got coming up…"

While **multitasking** is a big no-no for things that require concentration, it's perfect for relatively mindless tasks. Save time by paying bills or folding laundry when your favorite TV show comes on. Go jogging with a friend so you can socialize while staying fit. Check your friends' Facebook statuses while you're eating lunch. There are plenty of ways to kill two birds with one stone.

What with academics, extracurriculars, and jobs or internships, it can be hard to fit family and friends into your schedule. But making time for those who truly care about you will help keep you grounded. You can't do your best without a strong support network. In the same vein, don't forget to make time for yourself. Pencil in activities that make you happy, as well as time to just veg out. If you feel like you're getting overextended, remember that it's okay to say "no"—to a party, to an extracurricular, to an extra-credit assignment, to whatever it is that will completely swamp your schedule and wash you overboard.

In Their Own Words

"Spend time with family and friends. If you don't have the general feeling of well-being, you can't study well."

—Goldwater Scholar

"Don't neglect your needs as a balanced person. Make sure you see your friends [and] family and continue the activities that are important to you outside of school. Often you return to studying more refreshed and can concentrate better."

—Fulbright Scholar

"Make time for social things and fun [or] relaxing activities at least once per week."

—Top student

How Much Is Too Much?

Some people like to plan their schedule down to the hour. They designate 5 to 6 p.m. as history time, 6 to 7 as math time, 7 to 8 as dinner time, and so on. If this helps you stay on track, by all means plan away.

But in general, you don't need to micromanage your time. Although you *should* be aware of how much work you have for each subject, keeping your schedule flexible is better for a number of reasons:

- **Some assignments will take less time than you expect, others more.**
- **The amount of work for each class tends to fluctuate**. You may spend six hours studying for a class one week but only two hours the next.
- You should **study things as you're in the mood for them**. If you're tired, do something simple like proofreading an essay; when you're focused and alert, this is the perfect time to do math homework. (Of course, there are limits to this—if your algebra assignment is due tomorrow and you know it'll take all night, you'd better put your math hat on whether you want to or not!)
- If you get sick of one subject, you should be able to **move on to something else to perk up your brain**.
- **Stuff happens**. Your roommate invites you to a party; your mother calls; your Spanish teacher announces a quiz tomorrow; they're serving free pizza in the student lounge. Before you know it, several hours have passed and your schedule is totally obsolete.

If you still prefer the structure of an hourly agenda, you should create a new timeline each week—or better yet, each day. Don't force yourself into a fixed schedule all semester long. Treat your tasks as suggestions, not set in stone. An even better idea is to *give yourself an end time when you start each assignment*. For example, if you're sitting down to read a chapter from your bio textbook, tell yourself you're going to finish in an hour and a half. If you leave your study time open-ended, it has a tendency to drag on and on and on and on. You might even want to use a timer. Seeing the minutes ticking down like a bomb about to explode can be an excellent motivator.

In Their Own Words

"Set goals to finish a certain amount of material in [a] given time."

–High school valedictorian

Preventing Procrastination

Putting things off is a major problem among the school-age set. More than 70 percent of college students admit they're procrastinators, compared to about 20 percent of the adult population.[23] There are lots of reasons why people drag their feet. They may be bad at time management; they may be dreading the task; they may be perfectionists whose standards are so impossibly high that they're afraid to get started; they may be thrill-seekers who like the excitement generated by pushing the deadline; and so on. Whatever the case, procrastination can hold you back from getting the grades you want and deserve. Here are eight easy ways to stop procrastinating *now*.

1. **Break it up and be specific**. If a project is big and scary—like writing a research paper—getting started can be a struggle. You keep putting it off and putting it off, until finally you need an extension because you waited too long. Don't let this happen to you! Start by dividing the project into a series of smaller tasks, and write them down in the order you have to do them. Try to include deadlines for each one. Once you see it on paper, the job becomes much more approachable. Be as specific as you can about the steps—according to a 2008 German study led by Sean McCrea, people who think about projects in concrete terms are much more likely to do them than those who view them in the abstract.[24] So for a research paper, you should come up with something like this:

    a. Skim notes and textbook for potential topics. (Today)

    b. Do Internet research. (Tomorrow)

    c. Decide on topic. (Tomorrow or next day)

    d. Go to library and get out books on topic. (By end of this week)

    e. Read articles on JSTOR. (Over the weekend)

    f. Create research log. (Next week)

    g. Come up with thesis. (By end of next week)

    h. Do follow-up research. (Week of 10/15)

    i. Write outline. (Week of 10/15)

    j. Write paper. (Week of 10/15)

    k. Revise and get feedback. (Week of 10/22)

2. Remind yourself that **the project doesn't have to be perfect**. Do what you can the first time around, and fix it up later if you have the time.

3. **Don't keep it to yourself**. Tell a friend or even (gasp!) a parent what you're working on, and ask them to check up on you once in a while. Join a study group to be around others who have the same deadlines as you. Make your intentions public. For example, if you're in a dorm, write "Studying Econ!!!" on the whiteboard outside your door. When others expect you to do something, you're more likely to get off your butt and do it.

4. **The Ten-Minute Rule**. Tell yourself to work on something for ten minutes—what's ten minutes, after all?—and then see if you can keep going

5. **You don't have to begin at the beginning**. For example, if you're working on a paper and writing the intro is just too much pressure, start with the second paragraph instead.

6. If things in your room cause you to procrastinate, **head to a less distracting place**, such as the library.

7. Make a plan to **reward yourself** after you accomplish your task.

8. **Limit your use of websites that can zap your willpower**. Do you study your Facebook page when you should be brushing up on your Spanish? Do you tweet when you're supposed to be writing your paper on deconstructionism? If so, you may want to take the following radical steps: disconnect your Wi-Fi or simply turn your PC *off* when you don't have to use it. If you need assistance, use an app that can block your access to the Internet for a specific period of time, such as Freedom (http://macfreedom.com, for a fee), or that keeps you from going on social media sites and other websites you specify, such as Anti-Social for Macs (http://anti-social .cc) and SelfControl for both Macs and PCs (http://visitsteve .com/made/selfcontrol).

In Their Own Words

"Studying is, more than anything else, about discipline. I know that I'll be distracted if I study at home or with other people, so I study by myself in the library. I know I'll be distracted by the Internet, so I don't bring my laptop or I turn off the Internet. You don't need the discipline to resist distraction[s]; you just need the foresight to remove the potential distractions in the first place."

—Yale Law School student

Chapter 3
The Mind-Body Connection

High school and college students like to torture their bodies. They pull countless all-nighters, continually skip breakfast, eat nothing but ramen noodles for dinner, find creative new ways to guzzle alcohol, transform into couch potatoes, and gain 15 pounds at the freshman dinner buffet. At least, that's the stereotype. Hopefully you aren't guilty of all these behaviors. (I was guilty of one out of the six—I'll let you guess which one.) However, you may not be taking care of your body as well as you should, and this can have a serious impact on your grades. Your body and mind are not separate entities. You've got to pay attention to your health if you want your brain to function at full power. This is good news for all you students out there—it means that you can improve your grades simply by changing how you eat, sleep, and exercise.

How to Use Sleep to Maximize Your Learning Potential

One of the most challenging aspects of being a high school or college student is getting enough rest. Unfortunately, sleep deprivation is a common problem in schools across the country. Teenagers need a lot of sleep—between 8.5 and 9.25 hours per night—to feel rested, but only 15 percent reported getting that much on school nights, according to the National Sleep Foundation.[25] A 2010 study found that more than half of high school seniors have excessive daytime sleepiness, and that this makes it three times more likely for them to exhibit strong symptoms of depression.[26]

College students average six to seven hours of sleep per night, but most need more than eight hours to feel their best.[27] Not surprisingly, researchers have found a direct connection between lack of sleep and low grades. A 2001 study showed that college students who slept six hours or less per night had an average GPA of 2.74, while those with nine hours or more of quality sleep averaged 3.24.[28] (How they found enough people getting over nine hours a night, however, is beyond me.)

The Great Sleep Debate. There's some disagreement about how much sleep young adults really need. Federal guidelines recommend more than eight or nine hours, but a recent Brigham Young University study says that teenagers actually perform best with seven hours of shut-eye.[29] In other words, students need to sleep about nine hours to feel fully rested, but they may score better on tests if they get about two hours less. The bottom line is: do what works best for you. If you need more than seven hours to be at your peak, then sleep away. If you function just fine on seven, don't lie in bed for longer than you have to. But if you're getting less than seven, it may be time to take a nap!

As you've probably noticed, lack of sleep makes it harder to concentrate, think clearly, and remember things. It can cause you to feel grumpy and depressed, which in turn makes it more difficult to study. Getting a good night's sleep is also critical for your grades because that's when your brain does some of its best work.

According to the article "Quiet! Sleeping Brain at Work," by Robert Stickgold and Jeffrey Ellenbogen, "while we sleep, our brain is anything but inactive. It is now clear that sleep can consolidate memories by enhancing and stabilizing them and by finding patterns within studied material even when we do not know that patterns might be there." The researchers found that some aspects of people's cognitive processes improved only after a minimum of six hours of sleep. This unconscious state, they conclude, "does something to improve memory that being awake does not do."[30]

> **Survey Says**
>
> Most high achievers recognize the importance of sleep. Among them, 56 percent reported getting between six and eight hours of sleep per night in high school, while 31 percent got between eight and nine hours, and 13 percent between four and six. In college, the vast majority—71 percent—slept between six and eight hours. Another 18 percent got eight to nine hours of sleep, and 9 percent fell in the four-to-six-hour range.

This is good news for all you bleary-eyed students out there. You're not wasting time when you drift off to dreamland—you're actually getting smarter! You've probably experienced the miraculous effects of sleep before. When you come back to an activity you were learning the previous day—such as playing a piece on the piano or figuring out the derivative of a function—aren't you surprised at how you seem to have improved overnight? That's because your brain was hard at work while you were lying there like a lump.

Are you an owl or a lark? Studies have shown that high school students do better when classes start later, but that college students with early classes have higher GPAs than those who sleep in.[31] What's going on here? Do college students need less sleep than high schoolers? Not really. College students who avoid early classes seem to be more likely to drink lots of alcohol and have unhealthy sleep habits, which may be the real culprits. So if you like to get up with the sun, you may be at a slight advantage academically. But late risers take heart—if you stay away from the booze and consistently get a good night's sleep, you can catch just as many worms as the early birds.

Even if you're naturally an owl, you can transform into a lark when necessary. If you want to take an 8 or 9 a.m. class, try embracing the whole "early to bed and early to rise" thing. The key is to be consistent. Avoid taking naps, drinking caffeine, or exercising late in the day, so it'll be easier to hit the sack when the sun goes down. (Keep reading for more tips on how to fall asleep.) The real danger comes with the weekend, when your late-night habits can creep up on you. Try to go to sleep within an hour or two of your weekday bedtime, and set your alarm for a reasonable hour even when you don't have school.

Give Sleep More Priority

Many students underestimate the importance of sleep in their lives. When you've got a ton of work to do, you may feel like you can't afford to rest. The less you sleep, the more you'll get done, right? Well, maybe in the beginning, but soon you'll reach a point of diminishing returns. Your mind will drift; you won't retain as much; you'll read more slowly; and you won't make the connections you would if you were alert. It might take a couple of hours to do something that would ordinarily take you a fraction of the time. Remember that the less you sleep, the more your productivity suffers. I find that sleep has more effect on my mood, energy, and brainpower than anything else.

You shouldn't feel guilty about sleeping a "normal" amount—that is, seven to nine hours a day. A lot of students (and adults too, for that matter) like to brag about how sleep-deprived they are. Does this sound familiar to you?

Student 1: Oh man, I'm so tired.

Student 2: Me too, soooo tired.

Student 1: I could barely crawl out of bed this morning.

Student 2: I know. It took me, like, five cups of coffee before I could open my eyes.

Student 1: I only got, like, four hours of sleep last night.

Student 2: You're lucky. I only got two.

Student 1: Yeah, well, I've only gotten twenty hours of sleep this whole week.

Student 2: Really? I haven't slept more than ten, max.

Student 1: Dude, you're like a machine. How do you do it?

Student 2: [Head thudding on the desk.] Zzzzzzzzzzz.

This is what I call "competitive sleep-deprivation." Don't fall into the trap of skimping on sleep just because your friends are doing it. It's nothing to be proud of. Sleep is an essential activity that will improve your mood, sharpen your brain, give you more energy, and optimize your GPA.

In Their Own Words

"Get on a regular schedule. Sleep should be one of your highest priorities, especially with difficult subjects."

—Top student

Avoid All-Nighters like the Plague

Pulling all-nighters will make you feel horrible and create a sleep debt that will take you days, or even weeks, to pay back. A sleep debt, by the way, is the cumulative effect of missed sleep. You can't just go without rest for one night and return to your normal sleep patterns the next day; the hours you didn't sleep will come back to haunt you like an angry ghost until you make them up.

Your concentration, memory, and analytical skills will go down the tubes, although you may not even be aware this is happening. In a 1997 study, June Pilcher and Amy Walters found that college students who went without sleep for twenty-four hours performed significantly worse on a cognitive performance test than those who got about eight hours. Interestingly, when asked to complete a survey after the test, the sleep-deprived students rated their concentration level higher than the well-rested students did.[32] They didn't seem to realize that their brains were fatigued.

Every once in a while, staying up part or all of the night may be unavoidable. But most successful students don't do this more than a handful of times per semester. One of the worst things you can do is skip sleep the night before an exam; this is when your mind should be in prime working order. Plus, your brain needs a good night's sleep to absorb all the information you've been cramming into it.

> ## Survey Says
>
> In high school, 66 percent of top students never pulled an all-nighter, while 32 percent pulled between one and ten per term. In college, 34 percent of these students still avoided staying up all night, while 59 percent did it a couple of times a semester. All-nighters were even rarer before an exam: 95 percent said that they never stayed up all night if they had a test the following day in high school, and 64 percent never did so in college. (Another 18 percent said they did so "rarely.")

How to Fall Asleep

It's a horrible feeling when you toss and turn in bed at night, unable to fall asleep. A half hour passes, then an hour, then two hours, and you still are painfully awake. You know you need as much shut-eye as you can get, but your body just won't cooperate. Here are some tips on how to make the sandman come a little faster:

- **Use a sound machine** if you're troubled by loud neighbors or street noise. This little device has been a lifesaver for me, especially that year in college when I had a floormate who liked to play her music at full blast at three o'clock in the morning. (Ah, those were the days!) A good sound machine can play white noise (similar to static), sounds from nature (like a babbling brook or a seashore), and lots of other soothing melodies to block out ambient noise. Some alarm clocks come with built-in sound machines.

- Going to sleep is a lot like preparing for takeoff: **you must turn off all electronic devices**. Power down your computer, turn off your phone and TV, and dim the lights at least half an hour before going to sleep.

- **Don't take caffeine, exercise, or nap** for several hours before bedtime.

- Relax with a **warm bath or shower** at night.

- There's really something to the old trick of **counting sheep**, although any repetitive, simple pattern will do. I like to count numbers slowly in my head—the fluffy sheep are too distracting—and I'm usually passed out before I reach one hundred. Concentrating on counting helps block out worrisome thoughts, slows down your breathing, and puts you into a meditative, tranquil state.

- **Go to sleep around the same time every night**, including weekends, so your body doesn't get confused.

- **Read something dry and boring before going to bed.** This is an especially good time to memorize vocabulary, formulas, dates, and other facts you need for exams, as studies show that you remember things better when you learn them right before going to sleep.

- If you can't fall asleep within thirty minutes of lying down, **go and do something else**. I recommend reading a book in bed—the drier, the better. Whatever you do, don't lie there thinking about how much you need to go to sleep; this just makes insomnia worse.

- **Practice diaphragmatic breathing**, in which you inhale deeply with the muscles around your abdomen. This allows you to take in more air than you do with shallow chest breathing and tends to calm people down. Put your hands on your stomach and feel your belly rise each time you take a breath. Inhale gently through your nose, and let out each breath fully before you take another. Concentrate on slowing down your breathing.

- When you were a little kid, did your mom ever give you **warm milk** when you couldn't sleep? Well, moms know best, and this homey remedy has the power to send even the most hardened insomniac off to dreamland.

- Have a snack consisting of **rice, noodles, or grains**. These foods can boost levels of tryptophan, a chemical that induces sleepiness. Bananas are also quite soporific.

- **Melatonin** is a hormone produced by your pineal gland that helps regulate your sleep cycle. It's also a popular natural sleep aid that's available in pharmacies and health food stores. Read the label for instructions.

- If all else fails, **see a doctor**. Some underlying physical cause could explain your insomnia. Your doctor may prescribe something to help you rest or refer you to a center for sleep disorders.

Napping Is the New Normal

That's right, folks, naptime isn't just for babies anymore! According to a 2008 German study, as little as six minutes of shut-eye can boost your mental functioning and memory, while a thirty-five-minute nap is even more effective.[33] If you close your eyes for too long, however, you run the risk of falling into a deep sleep and waking up groggy and disoriented. This is called "sleep inertia." It often happens with naps lasting more than half an hour, so you may want to limit yourself to fifteen or twenty minutes. Everyone's sleep patterns are different, so you should experiment and find the duration that's right for you. A lot of high-profile companies are recognizing the benefits of power napping. Both Nike and Deloitte & Touche, for example, have provided quiet rooms for their employees.[34] It's like kindergarten all over again.

Word of warning: When you take naps at home, *make sure to set your alarm clock*. It's a nasty shock when you close your eyes for fifteen minutes and wake up to discover you've slept the whole day away. College students living on campus have the option of returning to their dorms for a quick siesta. If you're trying to sleep in a library or some other public place, consider using an eye mask and earplugs. It's a good idea to bring a watch or cell phone with an alarm, or even a travel alarm clock, for situations like this. Just remember to shut it off as soon as you wake up or put it on vibrate to avoid dirty looks from the librarians.

In Their Own Words

"I take short naps all the time—ten minutes here and there, anywhere."

—Yale Law School student

Study in the Morning Instead of at Night

There's no rule that says you must finish your work before bedtime. Why kill yourself staying up late when you can get the same amount of work done in a fraction of the time in the morning? I often went to bed early—between 8 and 10 p.m.—and woke up between 3 and 5 a.m. because I functioned much better after a good night's sleep.

Waking up before dawn to study takes willpower, but you get used to it. When you first get up, go about your normal morning routine—eat breakfast, have some coffee, exercise, watch a little TV, take a shower—to kick-start your brain. Studying in a straight-backed chair or standing up will help keep you awake.

You can also try studying in bed, although this is definitely not for everyone. I personally found it less painful to get up at three in the morning when I knew I could return to my warm, cozy blankets. Lying down was also more comfortable for me, which made it easier to concentrate for long periods of time; and it brought my face closer to what I was reading, making it harder for my eyes to wander.

The danger of studying in a horizontal position is, of course, that you may turn your books into pillows. It takes a combination of willpower and adrenaline to study effectively in bed, but it can be done. If you're experimenting with this, reset your alarm clock just in case you nod off. You can also take the edge off getting up early by telling yourself that you'll take a nap soon. Leave some time for a fifteen- or twenty-minute snooze after you've completed your work and before you have to head off to class.

If you don't want to take a nap or get up before dawn, there are plenty of other ways to stay alert. Try one (or more) of the following when you feel your eyelids getting heavy:

- **Do aerobic exercise** such as jumping jacks, jump-rope, or running. If you're physically able to, do a handstand or head-stand to get the blood flowing to your brain. It may feel silly, but it works!
- **Splash cold water on your face** to shock yourself into alertness.
- **Take a shower**.
- **Chat with a friend**.

- **Try working on something else** for a while. Your brain needs variety; concentrating on one book or subject for too long is bound to make you bored and sleepy.
- **Snack on brain-boosting foods**. (More on this later.)

Strategies for the Heavy Sleeper

Do you have problems getting up on time? Do you hit the snooze button repeatedly without realizing it? Does it take a minor miracle to wake you up in the morning? Here are six simple ways to get your butt out of bed.

1. Put your alarm clock far enough away that you have to get up and walk over to turn it off.

2. Have a back-up clock (such as a travel alarm) that will go off at the same time as your primary one.

3. Some clocks are louder than others. If you're sleeping through your current alarm, go shopping for one that can wake the dead.

4. If a screeching alarm clock isn't your thing, you might want to try a more humane machine. Hammacher Schlemmer's Peaceful Progression Wake Up Clock, for example, has lights that come on gradually as well as "stimulating aromas and peaceful nature sounds" to gently stir sleepers from their slumber.

5. Have your alarm go off fifteen to thirty minutes before you actually want to get up, so you can press the snooze button a couple of times. This gives your body time to accept that it's time to wake up.

6. Fill a spray bottle with water and put it on your night-table before you go to sleep. When the alarm goes off in the morning, spritz yourself in the face—you'll be out of bed in no time!

Caffeine: A Necessary Evil?

Ah, the age-old question: to caffeinate or not to caffeinate? My advice is to avoid it if you can. But, if you're a low-energy person (like me), caffeine can be helpful *in moderation*. I didn't start taking it until I was in college, by the way, so you can get great grades without relying on stimulants. Keep the following points in mind before you decide to add this drug to your diet:

- If you ingest too much caffeine, you could have side effects such as anxiety, rapid heart beat, nausea, insomnia, muscle tremors, increased urination, and many other unpleasant things (as I know from experience). How much is too much depends on the person, but it's generally more than 200 to 400 milligrams per day, or two to four cups of coffee.
- If you use caffeine on a regular basis, you will probably have to take increasingly larger doses to get the same effect. This is known as developing tolerance.
- Taking caffeine late in the day can throw you into a vicious cycle of insomnia → not getting enough sleep → needing more caffeine to compensate.
- Some unsubstantiated claims link caffeine to stunted growth and increased risk of osteoporosis, since it can affect your body's absorption of calcium.[35] To counter this, you should add milk to your coffee or drink a glass of milk every day.
- Excessive coffee consumption can irritate your stomach lining, leading to digestive disorders such as ulcers.
- Long-term coffee drinking may stain your teeth.

On the other hand, recent studies suggest that coffee may actually have some health benefits: coffee drinkers are less likely to have type-2 diabetes, Parkinson's disease, certain cancers, heart rhythm problems, and strokes.[36] Research has shown that caffeine improves memory and concentration.[37]

And don't forget about tea, coffee's less popular but more health-conscious cousin. Coffee generally contains more caffeine, but tea has a longer-lasting effect because its caffeine is released more slowly. The health benefits of tea, especially the green variety, are also remarkable—there's evidence that it helps prevent cancer and heart disease, among other things—so you might want to give tea a try before you start sipping the stronger stuff.[38]

The bottom line is: if you don't need caffeine, don't start. If you do start, take the smallest amount that improves your concentration for the shortest time possible to reduce your risk of dependence. It's also good to know how much caffeine you're actually getting on your coffee break (or at tea time, if you're so inclined).

Unfortunately, the caffeine content of some brand-name drinks is highly variable. A 16-ounce cup of joe from Starbucks may have about 100 milligrams more caffeine than the same serving size from Dunkin' Donuts, according to a study published in the *Journal of Analytical Toxicology*. The researcher also found that a cup of Starbucks coffee had 259 milligrams of caffeine in it one day, while a cup of the same size and flavor had 564 milligrams another day. Apparently all coffees are *not* created equal. Nevertheless, the following chart gives you a rough idea of what's in your drink (and, in some cases, food).[39]

The Amount of Caffeine in Drinks and Other Products	
Source	Caffeine (in milligrams)
Coffee	
Starbucks brewed coffee, 16 oz. (grande)	259–564
Dunkin' Donuts brewed coffee, 14 oz.	178

(continues)

The Amount of Caffeine in Drinks and Other Products, cont.

Source	Caffeine (in milligrams)
Coffee	
Starbucks espresso, 1 oz.	75
Generic brewed coffee, 8 oz.	95–200
Generic instant coffee, 8 oz.	27–173
Tea	
Black tea, 8 oz.	14–61
Green tea, 8 oz.	24–40
Herbal tea, 1 tea bag	0
AriZona iced tea, 8 oz.	11
Generic instant iced tea mix, unsweetened, 8 oz.	26
Lipton Brisk Lemon Iced Tea, 8 oz.	5–7
Soft Drinks	
7Up	0
Coca-Cola Classic	30–35
Diet Coke	38–47
Mountain Dew	46–55
Pepsi	32–39
Sprite	0
Other Products	
Monster Energy Drink, 8 oz.	80
Red Bull, 8.4 oz.	76–80
5-Hour Energy, 2 oz.	207
Excedrin, Extra Strength, 2 tablets	130
NoDoz (caffeine pill), 1 tablet	200
Haagen-Dazs coffee ice cream, 8 oz.	58

Sources: Energy Fiend (www.energyfiend.com), the Center for Science in the Public Interest (http://www.cspinet.org/new/cafchart.htm), and the Mayo Clinic website (http://www.mayoclinic.com/health/caffeine/AN01211).

Caffeine affects everyone differently, so you must decide how much works for you. In general, the smaller you are, the less caffeine you need. I'm 5'1" and weigh about a hundred pounds—in other words, I'm short and skinny. Since I disliked the taste of coffee, I would buy over-the-counter caffeine pills from the drugstore and cut them into quarters with a pill cutter. Each pill contained 200 milligrams of caffeine (the equivalent of one to two cups of coffee), and a quarter of a pill was usually enough to give me the boost I needed. Note that I did *not* just pop the whole thing in my mouth—if I did that, I would be bouncing off the walls like a kitten chasing the dot from a laser pointer.

During particularly busy and sleep-deprived periods, I might take the equivalent of two pills over the course of a day. More than that brought on a host of unpleasant side effects. By the way, the makers of caffeine pills say they're for occasional use only, although I've yet to come across any evidence that using them *in moderation* is any worse than drinking coffee. But if you're popping pills like a trucker on a midnight run, you may have a problem.

It's very important to know your body's reaction to caffeine before taking it on the day of an exam. The last thing you want is for your mind to be racing so fast in a caffeine-induced high that you can't even focus on the questions. And remember that you'll have adrenaline coursing through your body during the test, so you should adjust your dosage accordingly.

Energy drinks are all the rage among high school and college students, but think twice before you start chugging that can. By the time you reach the bottom, you may have met your sugar and caffeine quota for the day. Let's take a look at one 16-ounce can of Rockstar energy drink, which has about 60 grams of sugar and 160 milligrams of caffeine. That puts you way over the American Heart Association's recommended daily dose of about 24 grams of sugar for women and 36 grams for men.[40] As for caffeine, many people start experiencing negative effects from it at 200 milligrams. Plus, some drinks contain ingredients that amplify the effects of caffeine—such as guarana, which comes from a seed that's twice as potent as a coffee bean. If you do decide to imbibe, make sure you pay attention to the label. Some cans contain two or more servings, which means you're getting at least twice the dose that's listed on the back. If the label doesn't even tell you how much caffeine it has, give it a pass.

Study Drugs

A quick note about so-called "study drugs" such as Ritalin and Adderall: if these are not legally prescribed to you, *stay away*. First of all, you can get in serious trouble for taking them without a prescription—you might even be charged with a felony. Secondly, these are powerful drugs with lots of potential side effects, such as nervousness, insomnia, loss of appetite, nausea, dizziness, headache, drowsiness, stomach pain, high blood pressure, fatigue, chest pains, and mood changes. It's not a good idea to mess around with your brain chemistry, and dozens of deaths have been attributed to these drugs.

I took Adderall for a short time after it was prescribed to me by a doctor. At first, I thought it had potential. It made me feel like a super-student—extremely focused, energetic, and productive for long periods of time. However, my tolerance for it grew until I had to take twice the original dose to get the same effect, and I got terrible headaches when the drug wore off. I stopped taking it as soon as this happened and haven't looked back since.

You Are What You Eat (and Drink)

When I took the test to get into Stuyvesant, I made sure I ate an excellent breakfast that morning: scrambled eggs, toast, fruit, and a tall glass of orange juice. I didn't have much of an appetite, but I forced it all down anyway. For the first half of the exam, I felt great—alert, focused, and energetic. But then, at the end of the reading section, something happened that nearly ruined my chances of passing the test: I had to pee. I mean, I really, really had to pee. Like I was holding back Niagara Falls.

I usually don't drink anything at breakfast, and here I had gone and drunk a huge, cold, dripping glass of orange juice. For a long time I tried to ignore it, not wanting to spend precious minutes in the bathroom; but I could barely focus on the questions, and there came a point when I simply had to raise my hand and make a mad dash for the ladies' room. Fortunately I still managed to get into Stuyvesant, but just barely. The moral of the story is: don't drink a lot of liquid before a test. And more importantly, know how different foods and drinks affect you. The day of a major exam is *not* the time to experiment!

There's been a ton of research on what foods are good for the brain.[41] Growing up, I had a health-nut father who prevented me from falling into the many pits and traps of the typical American diet, but not everyone is so lucky. The following are some guidelines for a brain-friendly diet. It turns out that the foods that are good for your gray matter are also good for your body. Follow these rules, and you may end up with some welcome side effects: losing weight, having more energy, and living a longer, healthier life.

- **Rule 1: Keep your blood glucose level stable**. Fluctuations in blood sugar—a sugar rush followed by the inevitable crash—make it difficult for the brain to function properly. So how can you prevent this roller-coaster ride of highs and lows? Easy as…pineapple?

  - Avoid foods with simple sugars such as candy, cake, and cookies.
  - When you've got a sugar craving you can't shake, grab a piece of fruit. Strawberries, bananas, cherries, and peaches will satisfy your sweet tooth but are low in calories and high in vitamins, and take a long time to digest.
  - Drink water or tea instead of soda.
  - Use whole wheat bread for your sandwiches instead of the fluffy white variety, since whole grain is digested more slowly and is much more nutritious.
  - Legumes—foods such as peas, beans, lentils, carob, soy, and peanuts—can help you maintain a healthy blood sugar level.

  I'm not saying you can never eat junk food again—this will just make you bitter and cranky and less likely to stick to a high-brainpower diet—but reducing your sugar intake will help keep you from crashing. Think of sugar as the hare and complex carbs (such as legumes, vegetables, and grains) as the tortoise. As we all know, slow and steady wins the race.

- **Rule 2: Eat foods rich in iron and protein.** Iron helps transport oxygen to the brain; protein contributes to the production of neurotransmitters needed for alertness. Some good sources of iron are red meat, spinach, iron-enriched cereal (it should say so on the box), oysters, and beans. Just don't overdo it on the fatty meat, since this can cause health concerns such as high cholesterol. To provide for your protein needs, go for poultry, seafood, lean meats, and beans. The U.S.

Department of Agriculture (USDA) recommends between five and five and a half ounces of protein a day for young women, and about six and a half ounces for young men.[42] To give you a sense of what this means, an egg is about one ounce, and a small lean hamburger is about two to three ounces. For a fuller list of how much protein different foods contain, visit the USDA's website at www.choosemyplate.gov/food-groups /proteinfoods_counts_table.html.

- **Rule 3: Omega-3 fatty acids—a type of fat most common-ly found in fish such as salmon, sardines, and mackerel—can supercharge your synapses.** If you're not big on sea-food, you can get a potent dose of the stuff in fish-oil capsules, available at most pharmacies and health food stores. Grass-fed beef and pork, flaxseed oil (which you can use in your salad dressing), pumpkin seeds, and walnuts are also excellent sources of omega-3s.

- **Rule 4: Don't skip meals!** Studies show that students who eat a good breakfast do better in school than those who don't. As far as the brain is concerned, breakfast really is the most important meal of the day. And don't neglect lunch and dinner, either. Eating regular meals will help keep your blood glucose level stable.

- **Rule 5: Eat small snacks throughout the day to improve concentration.** It's awfully hard to focus on your physics lecture when you've got a growling stomach to contend with. To avoid this situation, eat super-smart snacks such as yogurt, nuts, cheese, and fruit. Apples are my ideal snack. They're cheap, tasty, and sat-isfying, and provide lots of energy without a subsequent crash.

- **Rule 6: Drink lots of water.** Your brain, which is over 80 per-cent water, is very sensitive to dehydration. Research has shown that just ninety minutes of sweating can cause your brain to shrink as much as a year of aging![43] But don't try to use this as an excuse for skipping your workout—drinking a glass or two of water will quickly restore your brain to its original size. Some health experts advise drinking six to eight glasses a day, but according to Margaret McCartney, MD, in the *British Medical Journal*, there's no need to over-saturate yourself—just drink water when you're thirsty.[44]

In Their Own Words

"Healthy eating is incredibly important—lots of fruits and vegetables. Stay away from frozen foods [and] foods out of a can."

—Goldwater Scholar

Menu from the Brain-Food Café

Here are a few suggestions for simple meals that will supercharge your brain. I'm not saying you *always* have to eat like this, although kudos to you if you do. I've certainly strayed far from the ideal diet. (Krispy Kreme donuts in the freshman cafeteria? I'm so there.) But you should try to develop brain-healthy eating habits. The more you do it, the easier it gets. Take special care to eat well in the week before a big project or exam. For the aspiring chefs among you, this is a great opportunity to come up with recipes that make your gray matter *and* your taste buds happy.

Breakfast Options:

- One or two eggs with whole-grain toast. The nutrients in egg yolks improve memory and cognitive function.
- A spinach and cheese omelet.
- Oatmeal or whole-grain cereal with fresh fruit.
- Plain yogurt with fresh fruit and nuts.
- Whole-grain bread with peanut butter.

Lunch Options:

- Salad with sesame seeds, vegetables, and strips of chicken.
- Veggie burger on a whole-grain bun.
- Whole-grain bread with peanut butter, and an apple.
- Plain yogurt with berries. Blueberries, which prevent inflammation in the brain and improve the way neurons communicate with each other, are one of the all-time best brain foods.
- Salmon with vegetables.
- Tuna fish sandwich on whole-grain bread.
- Fruit salad and cheese.
- Sushi.
- Bean burrito.

Snack Options:

- An apple and cheese.
- Nuts such as walnuts and almonds.
- Trail mix.
- Carrot sticks with hummus spread.
- Yogurt with berries and honey.
- Avocadoes—these fruits are full of monounsaturated fat, which improves blood flow to your brain.

Dinner Options:

- Salmon with brown rice and broccoli.
- Sushi with edamame (soybeans).
- Roasted chicken with corn and beans.
- Lean, grass-fed roast beef with lentil soup.
- Whole-grain pasta with cheese, spinach, and tomato sauce.
- Stir-fry with soybeans, broccoli, and brown rice.

- Salad with spinach, broccoli, and cauliflower, drizzled in flax-seed oil.

After-Dinner Dessert Options:

- Fresh fruit and walnuts.
- Dark chocolate. Researchers have found that the flavanols in dark chocolate boost blood flow to the brain for up to three hours.[45]
- Applesauce (with no added sugar).
- Ice cream with fresh fruit.
- Apple pie.

Drink Options:

- Water.
- Fruit juice with no added sugar. (You might even want to dilute with water to avoid a sugar rush.)
- Beet juice. Yep, you read that right. The nitrates in beets improve blood flow to the brain.
- Low-fat milk.
- Coffee (not advisable at dinner time).
- Tea.
- Note that soda is *not* on the menu.

What Would You Like with Your Exam?

Most nutritionists are concerned with the foods you eat outside the classroom, but they ignore an important strategy for getting better grades: consuming high-energy snacks *during* exams. I would never have been a top student without this. Some teachers forbid you to eat and drink in their presence. If that's the case, don't make them angry by trying to sneak in supplies. But if they're okay with it, go ahead and feed your brain while you're circling answers and scribbling out essays.

I often felt like I was about to lapse into a coma in the middle of an exam. The questions stopped making sense; I couldn't maintain my train of thought; and everything I had studied seemed to fly out the window. It was then that I whipped out my secret weapons: apple slices and string cheese. These snacks helped bring my brain back from the dead, thus saving me from academic oblivion.

Good exam foods have the following qualities: they're tasty, easy to eat, and transportable; they're not messy or smelly; they don't require forks, knives, or spoons; they can be eaten with one hand; they're healthy, simple, and filling; and they don't make you crash. You shouldn't do anything that takes concentration, like peeling an orange or digging around in a salad. You *should* be able to read and answer test questions while nibbling on your snack. Avoid simple sugars like candy, cakes, and cookies, although these may be the most readily available foods in your school's vending machines. I always came prepared with my own snacks. In my experience, the four best test foods are:

1. **Apples**. High in fiber, this fruit gives me hours of energy and is remarkably filling. Before your test, cut up an apple and put the slices in a plastic bag to make it easier to eat.

2. **Fruit leather**, also known as fruit strips or fruit rolls. These are basically whole servings of fruit steamrolled into the thickness of a quarter. They're much easier than regular fruit to eat and transport—and tasty, too. Make sure you get the kind that's all fruit, no added sugar. I recommend the ones made by Stretch Island.

3. **String cheese**. Cheese snobs may scoff, but I like these plastic tubes of mozzarella because they're transportable and easy to eat. String cheese is a good source of protein, and you can eat it in under a minute if you bite it instead of pulling it off in strings.

4. **Fruit and nut bars**. It's like eating a candy bar, only they're

made of—you guessed it!—nuts and dried fruit. Again, avoid the ones with added sugar. I like the bars made by a company called Kind, available in many supermarkets and health food stores.

You might also want to bring trail mix (nuts and raisins), water (to prevent dehydration), and coffee or tea. Make sure your drink is in a closed container to prevent a fluid faux-pas. Before the exam, put your snacks and drinks in easy-to-reach places so you don't have to go searching for them later. This would be disruptive to you and your classmates, and rifling through your backpack in the middle of an exam could bring unwelcome attention from your professor.

How to Prevent Food Comas

You've probably experienced this before. You sit down to a magnificent feast and can't wait to dig in. You shovel food into your mouth like Garfield on a lasagna rampage, and your stomach rejoices. Finally, you're full. A few minutes pass, and then it hits you: the dreaded food coma. All you want to do is close your eyes and pass out on the table.

Food comas—known as postprandial somnolence by people who liked to get beaten up during recess—are fine when you're relaxing with friends or family, but they're a major setback when you have exams and papers to write. (By the way, turkey has no more tryptophan—a chemical that induces sleepiness—than chicken and beef, so don't blame the bird next time you doze off on Thanksgiving. The real reason people lose consciousness on this holiday is simply that they eat too much!)

So how do you avoid feeling sluggish after a meal? Rule Number One: *Don't stuff yourself!* Eating until you're ready to burst isn't good for your body or your brain. To avoid overeating, have small snacks throughout the day so you don't gobble down your food at mealtime.

Eat slowly so your stomach has time to register its fullness. Foods that take time or effort to eat—such as salad, unshelled nuts, and shellfish—are especially good at forcing you to slow down. Drinking coffee or tea with your meal can help cancel out the effects of a coma.

You should also *go for a walk or do some other light exercise* (jumping jacks, running in place) after you eat to get your blood moving. Bend over forward so your head is below your heart, forcing blood to your brain. Remember: Gravity is your friend. And if food fatigue does strike, take a quick nap. Go back to your dorm room and set your alarm for fifteen minutes, or find a quiet corner in the library and put your head down. You'll wake up feeling as good as new.

Exercise for Your Brain

It should be clear by now that what's good for your body is good for your brain, and exercise is no exception. Many studies show a positive correlation between physical activity and academic performance.[46] For example, at Naperville Central High School, students who took PE immediately before a reading class improved twice as much as those who didn't move around.[47] Another study has shown that twenty minutes on the treadmill can improve students' problem-solving abilities.[48] Exercise increases blood flow to the brain, so it makes sense that physical activity will boost your concentration. Perhaps just as importantly, exercise elevates your mood, making it easier to stay upbeat and focused.

How Much?

An hour a day of moderate physical activity is ideal. If that's not possible, try doing a half-hour each day or every other day—a little is better than nothing at all. Studies have shown that twenty to thirty minutes of physical activity are enough to improve mental performance. If you're already on a sports team at school, congrats; you're probably all set in this department. If not, find a sport or activity that you truly enjoy and stick with it. It can be team-oriented or independent, organized or unstructured, as long as it gets you moving.

When to Do It?

Since exercise improves your mood and concentration, it's best to do it early in the day, before your classes. Another good time is before settling down to do your homework. However, be careful about exercising so strenuously that you're too exhausted to think. If you can't concentrate when you're sweaty, give yourself enough time to shower before getting down to business. When you're studying or doing homework, take a break every hour or so for a short burst of physical activity such as jumping jacks, stretching, and running in place.

In Their Own Words

"Exercise is incredibly important. It allows you to relax and de-stress.... I work out every day, even if I'm preparing for an exam. I think working out is one of the keys to doing well....It kept me sane."

—Goldwater Scholar

Exercises

Exercise 1:

Sometimes our daily habits can affect us in ways we aren't even aware of. This exercise will help you keep track of and evaluate your sleep, diet, and physical activity—and figure out how to improve them!

Step 1: On separate pieces of paper, answer the following questions every day for the next two weeks. See if you notice any patterns. For example, does your energy level plummet when you sleep less than seven hours? Do you wake up from a half-hour nap feeling groggy or alert? Does your concentration suffer or improve when you eat certain foods?

Tip: Engage in physical activity for at least half an hour a day to supercharge your brain.

How much sleep did you get last night?

____ hours

What did you have for breakfast?

_____

_____

What did you have for lunch?

_____

_____

What did you have for dinner?

_____

_____

If you had any snacks, what were they?

_____

_____

How much caffeine did you have today? (For example, if you drink coffee, write down the number of cups.) _____

If you took a nap today, how long was the nap?

___ hours ___ minutes

How did you feel after the nap (groggy, alert, etc.)?

_____

_____

How much did you exercise today?

___ hours ___ minutes

On a scale of 1 to 10, rate your energy level today: ___

On a scale of 1 to 10, rate your ability to concentrate today: ___

Step 2: At the end of two weeks, write down five observations about how your physical habits influence your mental functioning. (For example, half-hour naps make me groggy, but fifteen-minute naps help me focus; my energy level goes down when I don't exercise; I couldn't concentrate on days when I skipped breakfast.)

1. _____

_____

2. _____

_____

3. _____

_____

4. _____

_____

5. _____

_____

Exercise 2:

List three specific things you can do to achieve a more brain-friendly diet—for example, eating a good breakfast, bringing healthy snacks to school, and cutting out soda.

1. _____

_____

2. _____

_____

3. _____

_____

CHAPTER 4
How to Play the Game (Navigating Academia)

B EING A SUCCESSFUL STUDENT is about more than reading, writing, and 'rithmetic. It's about being a skilled negotiator, a keen observer, and a master planner. It's about figuring out what your courses require and how your teachers think—and let's not forget about your TAs. It's about avoiding the bad classes (and bad teachers) as much as possible, but also knowing how to deal when you can't. In this regard, it helps to think of school as a game—and like any game, it can be won with enough practice, skill, and strategy.

Game Strategy 1: Be Smart about Your Schedule

If you're in college, you probably have to plan your schedule every term. Choosing your classes can be exhilarating, but it's also a big responsibility. The courses you choose can mean the difference between an A+ semester and the term from hell. To keep your schedule under control, start with the classes you need to fulfill your school's graduation requirements and your major requirements, if you've declared one, and then round your schedule out with electives.

Aim for a good mix of subjects to keep the term interesting. Sign up for a few advanced classes if you're qualified for them, along with some mid-level and intro ones. Unless you want to live in the library, don't take more than two or three extremely reading-intensive or research-driven classes per term. And if you haven't declared a major yet, this is the perfect time to try subjects you may have never considered—or even heard of—before.

Shop Smart

One of the best things about college is that you get to test-drive your classes before you buy them. In this so-called "shopping period," students sign up for way more classes than they actually need, sit in on them for a week or two, and then drop the ones they don't like. Even if you think you know exactly what classes you want to take, it's a good idea to check out a few extras. You may find that you can't stand the professor of that English class you had your heart set on and need a replacement *stat*.

A lot depends on the decisions you make in this brief span of time, so you've got to play it smart during your shopping spree. Make sure you *pay attention to pre-reqs*—don't waste your time check-ing out a course where you'll be in over your head. You should *attend the first and second meeting of every class you're considering*. On the first day, the teacher will probably distribute the syllabus, discuss grading policies, and go over the scope of the course; but he or she may not actually start lecturing until the second meeting. Knowing what the class will cover is one thing, but deciding whether you like the prof's teaching style is a whole other ball game. Even if you're not sure whether you're going to keep a class, *take notes as you normally would*. If you do decide to stick with it, you'll be grateful for those notes later.

In addition to sitting in on classes, *read reviews of the teachers* on www.ratemyprofessors.com, or see if students from your school have set up their own online forum. Take these reviews with many grains of salt, however, as students with a grudge against the teacher are more likely to submit comments. Also ask your friends what they know about the classes you're considering. If there's a cap on enrollment, *drop the course or inform the teacher, or both, as soon as you decide not to take it*, as other students may be waiting to sign up. That's just good karma.

For each class you're considering, ask yourself the following questions:

- Do you like the teacher?
- Is he or she easy to understand?
- Do the topics interest you?
- Can you handle the workload?

You've got to trust your instincts on this—no matter what the online reviews or your friends say, your views take precedence. Remember, though, that it's not always as simple as dropping the classes you don't like; you've got to make sure you're fulfilling requirements, too. Sometimes, in order to do this, you may have to pick the least bad courses rather than the ones you like best.

Some large lectures will require you to join a **discussion section** (also known as recitation) that meets outside of class time, which you may or may not have to register for separately. Typically led by a TA (teaching assistant), recitations give you the opportunity to discuss the lecture or readings in a small, intimate setting, much like a seminar. While discussion sections can be rewarding, they can also tack a lot of extra time onto your schedule without this being shown on your transcript. It's like you're taking a seminar but only getting credit for a lecture.

As the shopping period comes to an end, *plan your final schedule carefully*. To preserve your sanity, try not to take more than two classes in a row. Make sure you have enough time to get from class to class—having to sprint every day to make that lecture all the way across campus gets old fast. In some schools, it's possible to fit all your classes into four days and have Friday free. The beginning of your week may be jam-packed, but having a three-day weekend more than makes up for it. Finally, at the end of the shopping period, make sure you've officially dropped the classes you decide not to take! Otherwise you may be in for a *very* unpleasant surprise when your transcript arrives at the end of the semester.

> **Survey Says**
>
> Most top students do not overload their schedule. The majority took five or fewer classes per term (based on a typical two-semester academic year). Among these students, 48 percent had an average of five classes per semester; 36 percent took four; 9 percent took six; and only 7 percent took more than six.

How many classes should you take? Unless you're determined to graduate early, it's better not to overload your schedule. In general, the fewer courses you have, the more you'll get out of them and the better you'll do. You can spend more time reading the material, practicing problems, resolving issues, and getting to know your professors. When deciding your schedule in the beginning of the term, remember that you may be able to handle the workload initially, but once midterms roll around, you'll regret having taken that extra class in twentieth-century Swedish film.

Game Strategy 2: Get in Step with STEM

STEM has been in the news a lot these days—and no, I'm not talking about stem cells or the study of plants. In this case, STEM stands for science, technology, engineering, and math—majors that are very much in demand in today's job market, but which have serious trouble retaining students. More than 60 percent of entering college freshmen who plan to major in these fields wind up graduating with a non-STEM degree, according to *Engage to Excel*, a 2012 report by the President's Council of Advisors on Science and Technology.[49]

This raises some big questions, such as: Why is it so hard to stick with STEM, and what can you do to improve your chances if you decide to go into one of these fields? Let's take a closer look at what STEM is, what special challenges its students face, and how you can successfully navigate this maze of atoms, algorithms, and animal dissections.

Grade Inflation?

What's that? When economics professor Kevin Rask analyzed the GPAs of approximately 5,000 graduates from an unnamed Northeast liberal arts college, he made some startling discoveries. Chief among them was the inequality of grades between STEM and non-STEM majors. According to Rask, "all the STEM departments fall below the college mean," with five of the six lowest-grading departments belonging to STEM. Plus, intro courses in science, technology, engineering, and math are "among the lowest grading courses on campus."[50]

In the school Rask studied, chemistry (with an average grade of 2.78), math (2.90), economics (2.95), psychology (2.98), and biology (3.02) are the lowest-graded subjects, while religion (3.22), music (3.30), English (3.33), language (3.34), and education (3.36) make up the top five. (Economics is the only non-STEM major in the sub-3.0 category, although there's some debate over whether psychology should be considered STEM.)

Some people claim this is because science, tech, engineering, and math are harder than the humanities, but I think it's more accurate to say that the STEM majors are graded harder. The humanities aren't innately easier; they just have more grade inflation than STEM. I've known plenty of students who were extraordinary in math and science, but who couldn't write a paper or analyze a book to save their life. And I had more overall work as a history student than as a computer science major because of the endless amounts of reading, writing, and research required by the former.

Warning: Dangerous Curves Ahead

One of the reasons for STEM's lower GPAs is a practice that has inspired fear and loathing among generations of college students. I'm talking about *The Curve*. Not all STEM classes have it, but it's much more common there than in the humanities. According to this philosophy, only a certain percentage of the class is allowed to get As, Bs, Cs, and so on. Teachers may decide that a set number will fail before the term has even started!

In effect, a student's grade is based more on how he or she does compared to everyone else than on any objective measure of performance. In some classes, students may get decent grades on tests but still find themselves barely scraping by on their report card. Others may make huge improvements over the course of the term, only to wind up with a dismal grade because their overall performance didn't match up to that of their peers. Not surprisingly, this can make for an extremely tense, competitive, and cutthroat environment.

Having a curve isn't all bad, though. For example, an abysmal test score doesn't necessarily mean the end of the road. I've had some computer science tests where the average was in the 30s or 40s (yes, that's out of 100), which meant that a 50 might put you in the A range. In most cases, your teacher will tell you what the average is so you know how you're doing. The scariest classes are those where you're kept in the dark until report-card time. Here are some tips for how to deal with a major where curving is a way of life:

- **Make sure your teacher gets to know you**. Go to his or her office hours, volunteer in class, send emails, and so on. If you're on the fence between grades at the end of the semester, this will often help push you over the edge.

- **Go to your TA's help sessions as often as possible.** The teaching assistant may give away advice and insider information that will mean the difference between beating the curve and getting crushed under it.

- **Plan your schedule carefully.** Some classes appeal to geniuses and grad students who will set the bar very high. Others attract students with a wider range of backgrounds and abilities, making it much easier to beat the curve. You can't always avoid the super-hard classes, but you should try to arrange your schedule so you get a good mix.

- For each exam, **always write down the average test score** and any other information your teacher gives you, so you don't lose track of how you're really doing.

- Do all **extra credit assignments**, unless they interfere with your regular schoolwork.

- Accept the fact that you might not do as well as you'd like and try not to stress out about it too much. If STEM is really what you want to do, don't worry if your GPA is lower than that of your English major roommate. **The best advice I can give you is not to pick your major based on GPA.**

Sink or Swim

Unfortunately, some STEM programs are guilty of a "sink or swim" mentality, in which students from all different educational backgrounds are thrown into a sea of challenging courses with little or no support from the faculty. Many students, feeling in over their heads, will change majors or even drop out of school. On the bright side, some schools are trying to welcome more students into STEM. For example, Harvey Mudd's computer science program has taken steps to attract and retain female students, who normally steer clear of the subject (currently only 18 percent of CS undergrads are women), and the school now has an intro course for students with no prior programming experience. No matter what kind of program you're in, the following tips will help you stay afloat in STEM:

- Try to find at least one faculty member in the department who will serve as **a mentor**. This should be a person you feel comfortable with and who can give you lots of advice and encouragement.
- A key indicator of success in STEM is **preparation in high school**—so if you're in the pre-college crowd, take lots of advanced classes in science and math. That will help you decide whether you like one of these fields, and you'll enter college with a big advantage.
- If you're deciding where to go to college, **speak with faculty and students** in the department(s) you're interested in. Feel them out on how competitive the classes are, whether students are happy, and whether the profs are supportive of the students.
- **Have a backup plan**. If your intended major turns out not to be a good fit, know what your options are. Could you do a minor instead of a major? Does the department offer a related major that would allow you to take a wider variety of courses? When is the latest you could switch your major and still graduate on time? Keep in mind that some schools offer a BA *and* a BS in STEM disciplines, and going for the BA version may give you more flexibility.

Another reason why many students fear STEM is that it's cumulative. Everything is built on what comes before it, so if you get stuck or lost on a topic, your grades can go downhill fast. Cognitive science expert Donald Norman put it best when he said that the typical mathematics curriculum "continues relentlessly on its way, each new lesson assuming full knowledge and understanding of all that has passed before. Even though each point may be simple, once you fall behind, it is hard to catch up. The result: mathematics phobia."[51]

That's why, if you're having trouble with a topic in STEM, you'd better get help quickly—from a teacher, a TA, a tutor, or even a study group. The sooner you clear up your difficulty, the less trouble you'll have down the road. Non-STEM courses are very different in that you can jump in at pretty much any point and figure out what's going on. That's not to say there's no progress in majors like English and history—you will gain knowledge and become a better writer, reader, researcher, critical thinker, and so on. But if you join a math or science class without the necessary prerequisites, you may wonder why people are suddenly speaking in a foreign language!

Yet another reason why STEM can be intimidating is its lack of leeway. While most humanities classes welcome interpretation, opinion, and debate, in math the answer is either right or wrong. In computer science the code either works or it doesn't, and so on. How you react to this state of things largely depends on your personality. If you're a stickler for certainty, you might be a good candidate for STEM. If you prefer subjectivity and differing points of view, you may be a humanities person at heart. Keep in mind, though, that you can get partial credit in most math and science classes, and creativity and imagination are valued in STEM, just in a different way.

Many STEM students—especially those in engineering—have been missing out on a well-rounded college education. Only 21 percent of engineers had substantial amounts of coursework encouraging understanding of other cultures, according to the 2011 National Survey of Student Engagement.[52] Another study, by Alexander Astin, found that majoring in engineering is associated with a decline in writing ability, cultural awareness, and political participation.[53] This may be due to the extensive number of pre-reqs and requirements necessary for an engineering degree, leaving little time for pursuing that interest in nineteenth-century Italian opera. If you're a wannabe engineer still applying to or deciding on a college, find out how much time undergrads have to take classes outside their major. If you're already in an engineering program, consider taking some of your classes in the summer so you have more time to try new things. Remember that employers like well-rounded people. You can score lots of career points by having skills like writing and knowledge of a foreign language.

Game Strategy 3: Know Thy Class

Throughout college, I saw the same three types of classes again and again. These categories have little to do with the subject or level of the class; they're based on what you're being graded on and how to prepare for each one. Of course, not every class will fall into one of these three groups, but the majority will. Sometimes you'll realize what kind of class it is after a few exams; other times your teacher will tell you what to expect or spell it out in the syllabus.

1. **Classes where you can pretty much ignore the readings**. Your teacher is testing you exclusively on what he or she says in class; if it's not in the lecture, it won't be on the exam.

   How to handle it—Go to every class, take extremely good notes, and make sure you know those notes forward and backward. But guess what: for the most part, you don't have to do the readings! The main exceptions are if you're expected to discuss them in class or write something about them. This kind of class can be a lifesaver in semesters when you're up to your eyeballs in work.

2. **Classes where you can pretty much ignore the lecture.** You won't be tested at all on what happens in class. This isn't as common as the previous one, but it can happen—for example, if your grade is based exclusively on one or two research papers.

    How to handle it—Go to class every day if attendance is taken, if you have to participate, or if it's a small class where you will be missed. Otherwise, feel free to skip it once in a while, just not so much that you lose touch with what's going on. (Yes, that's right. I said you can skip class—under certain conditions!) Pay attention in class, but keep your notes short and sweet. If you have to do research papers, you should be listening for ideas on what to write about and your teacher's expectations.

3. **Classes where you must know both the readings and the lecture extremely well.** There's not a lot of overlap and you'll be tested on both, so pretty much everything you see or hear is fair game.

    How to handle it—These killer classes can really eat up your time, so try not to take too many of them per semester. There's no way to cut corners: to succeed, you've got to have near-perfect attendance, take excellent notes, and do all the required readings. These classes are often the ones that you'll look back on with the greatest sense of accomplishment—although you may not feel this way at the time!

Game Strategy 4: Know Thy Teacher

Besides getting to know your classes, you've got to know your teachers! More often than not, they'll fit into one of these five categories.

1. The perfect teacher who gives interesting lectures, easy home-work, and fair tests, and is a generous grader to boot.

2. The teacher who gives interesting lectures but unfair tests, and who has apparently never heard of grade inflation. You like this teacher at first—until the grading begins.

3. The teacher who gives painfully dry or confusing lectures but easy tests. You initially can't stand him or her, but your feelings turn to love, or at least forgiveness, when you see your grades.

4. The all-around terrible teacher who presents boring or con-fusing lectures, gives unfair or extremely difficult tests, and is a merciless grader.

5. The misunderstood teacher. They may be tough on the out-side, but deep down they're all soft and mushy. You've heard horror stories about this person, but you find they're mostly untrue when you take the class. As long as you do the work, this prof is actually pretty fair.

Getting to know your teachers—understanding what they think, how they grade, and what their expectations are—is crucial to aca-demic success. One of the best ways to do this is by paying close attention in the classroom. But you should also make an effort to get to know teachers after class. Go to their office hours, send them emails, and talk to them after class if there's time. Of course you shouldn't make a nuisance of yourself, but if you have legitimate questions or concerns, don't hesitate to make them known.

This interaction has two main purposes: (1) you gain insight into how your teachers think and what might show up on exams, as well as getting your questions answered; and (2) teachers get to know you, which can often lead to them raising your final grade, giving you a letter of recommendation, and lots of other good stuff.

In Their Own Words

"If you have any questions, don't be afraid to talk to the teacher or professor. Spending time in office hours was one of the most helpful things I did. It not only helps with the class, but can lead to helpful letters of recommendation."
—Rhodes Scholar and 2010 NCAA Woman of the Year

"Getting to know the professor, knowing what they like and don't like in terms of methodology/ideas, helps a lot (in the context of liberal arts classes)."
—Yale Law School student

"It's...important to listen to the instructor to determine what he [or] she considers important."

—PhD in mathematics

Unfortunately, you will encounter some terrible teachers in your academic career. Some will be boring or unclear; others may be downright mean. If they're boring, you usually just have to suck it up. If they're unclear, your textbook has just become your new best friend—and if that's not enough, consider joining a study group. If teachers are mean, treat them like a bomb that could go off at any second and take extra care not to get on their bad side.

The worst teachers are those who are downright unfair. They don't test you on what they say they will, or they're too harsh on your papers, or their test questions are about twenty times harder than anything you did in class or for homework. In these situations, you should raise your concerns with the teacher—politely, of course—and ask your classmates if they feel the same way. They may open your eyes to something you've been missing or give you advice on how to do better. If it's still not enough, consider getting a tutor.

The Truth about TAs

In college, never underestimate the power of teaching assistants. They can make your class a wonderful experience or lead you to vow never to take that subject again. This is especially true in STEM, where they're often the first people you go to for help. In some classes, they will be the ones giving you your grade, not the professor. If you have a discussion section, you'll probably get to know your TA far better than you know your prof. So it's important to know how to handle these individuals caught in that awkward stage between student and teacher.

If you can choose your TA, shop around in the beginning of the semester. Go to their office hours or discussion sections and feel them out. Trust your instincts: a good TA will try to help instead of treating you like a pest, and he or she will be clear and easy to understand. Sometimes your TA will be a student who took the class last term and did really well. If that's the case, ask if they have any tips about the class or the teacher. They may be bursting with good advice.

This should go without saying, but make sure you treat your teaching assistant with respect. For example, if you schedule a meeting with your TA to go over a test, don't stand him or her up like a bad date! At the same time, remember that TAs are far from infallible. I've had several who were flat-out wrong about subject matter and requirements. Don't expect their mistakes to save your butt come grading season. If you suspect your TA is wrong, proceed up the chain of command to your professor.

In Their Own Words

"See TAs before exams. Often they will strongly hint as to what questions are on it. They also do the grading, so if they know you they are more likely to give you a higher grade."

—College valedictorian

Game Strategy 5: Appeal a Grade

You may think you're done when you hand in an exam or homework assignment. You did your best, and it's out of your hands. What you get, you get. But actually, there's one thing left to do: when you get your work back, it's your responsibility to make sure it was graded correctly. (I know this may be hard to believe, but teachers and TAs have been known to make mistakes!) You should never be afraid to challenge a grade if you have good reason, such as:

- Something was misgraded or miscalculated. Your teacher will have to give it to you on this one.
- You find something in your books or notes that contradicts the test-maker's answer.
- You explain how the question can be misinterpreted. This one's iffy, but it's worth a shot.
- The question asked you about something that the syllabus or your teacher expressly stated would *not* be on the exam.
- The grader didn't understand what you were trying to say on an essay question. You'll have to show that's the case.

Remember that disputing a grade does **not** make you a grade-grubber. A grade-grubber is someone who sucks up to get better marks; you're just fighting to get what you deserve.

Appealing a Final Grade

The term's finally over, and you're about to start a much-needed vacation. You get your report card, expecting some pretty great marks, and suddenly your jaw drops. "That can't be right," you think. "There must be some mistake." One of your grades is the wrong letter of the alphabet! So what should you do? Disputing a score on a test or assignment is one thing; challenging a final grade is another.

But take heart! The marks on your transcript are not set in stone. If you're convinced your final grade is not what it should be, act fast, because most schools have a time limit on when you can appeal your grade. Schedule an appointment with your teacher if you're not sure how he or she came up with the final grades. If the class is curved, this could make it awfully confusing.

Have You Seen Your Final Exam?

A lot of teachers won't return your final exam to you, but you typically will be allowed to see it if you make an appointment. (Think of this as visitation rights for your final.) After all, how do you know something was graded properly if you don't even look at it? Bring a calculator so you can quickly add up the points, and review your answers with the teacher. If you're lucky, you'll find something was misgraded or misinterpreted. Sometimes, your teacher will agree to give you a few extra points if you verbally explain how to answer a question, even if you got it wrong on the exam. (This happened to me once in college, and I *did* get my final grade changed!)

Make Sure That All Your Grades Were Included

One time in high school, I averaged my test and project scores and realized that my final grade was much lower than it should have been. When I raised this point with the teacher, he found that one of my grades hadn't been recorded—an honest mistake, but one that could have cost me the valedictorian spot if I hadn't caught it! (In case you were wondering, you should always hold on to your tests, projects, and homework assignments until the end of the semester.)

Be Professional

If things aren't going your way when you're appealing a grade, don't get angry—and definitely do not accuse the professor of disliking you or being a bad teacher. This will just put him or her on the defensive. Be courteous and respectful, and chances are your teacher will do the same.

Take It to a Higher Power

If, after discussing your grade with your teacher, you still believe that your work was not graded fairly—or if you attribute your low grade to racism or sexism or some other form of discrimination—you may be able to submit an appeal to the department or school officials. Speak with a dean or guidance counselor about your options, and look up your school's policy on the Web. Do *not* take this lightly, however. It's a serious step that could get your teacher in trouble, and it might not give you the best reputation among the faculty.

Chapter 5
In the Classroom

WHENEVER I MISSED SCHOOL and borrowed my classmates' notes, I was shocked by what I saw—or rather, what I didn't see. The pages were practically blank! They had written maybe half a dozen lines during the entire lecture, which took me less than a minute to jot down. The people who asked to borrow my notes, however—and let me say, I got *a lot* of requests—didn't get off so easily. They had to pay a visit to the local copy machine and scrounge around for loose change before they could get my notes. By the time they finished, they had a five- to ten-page (or sometimes longer) booklet from which they could reconstruct yesterday's class. Now I ask you: who got the better deal?

As you can probably tell, I'm a big believer in the value of note-taking. Throughout my academic career, one of the most important things I did was take good notes in class. During some lectures I would write pretty much nonstop, scribbling away so furiously that my hand felt like it was about to fall off by the end. (Don't worry, that feeling goes away after a minute or two.)

Why are good notes so critical, you may ask? Because most teachers take a majority of their test questions directly from their lectures. I'll turn the caps lock and bold font on, just so you know

I'm serious: **MOST TEACHERS TAKE A MAJORITY OF THEIR TEST QUESTIONS DIRECTLY FROM THEIR LECTURES**. The better your notes are, the easier it is to do well on exams. Am I saying you should write down everything the teacher says? Not at all—this is almost as bad as writing six lines for the entire lecture—but taking thorough, detailed, comprehensive notes has the potential to transform your GPA.

And here's an even bigger reason to take good notes—it can drastically cut down your study time. I know it might seem counter-intuitive because more notes mean more stuff to review, right? But actually, it's just the opposite. Having detailed notes means that you won't have to spend as much time studying other things. Most of the material you'll need to know will be right there in your notebook, in a compact and easily readable format, so you can devote less time to deciphering your textbooks.

How to Take Killer Notes (Hint: Less Isn't Always More)

Great notes require three things: speed, thoroughness, and clarity. In general, you should try to record every point, big or small, from your lectures. Lots of students make the mistake of writing down only the Really Big Ideas. But guess what—nothing your teachers say is off limits come test time. While they're more likely to quiz you on the major issues, they'll also throw in some stuff you thought you'd never see again, just to keep you on your toes. Plus, it's important to know how the big ideas relate to the smaller points and factual details that make up the rest of the lecture.

As you take notes, you should also be thinking about how the material might show up on tests. People, dates, definitions, and other facts are prime fodder for multiple-choice questions and short answers. You'll probably have to write about the main ideas in essays and use sub-points and facts to back up your arguments. And make sure you know how to solve every problem discussed in math and science classes. You can expect to see variations of them on the exam!

Be an undercover classroom reporter. When you take notes, pretend you're a reporter at a press conference. The goal is to record enough information to write an article on what you just heard. You need to know what the main points are and how they tie together, plus lots of juicy facts to keep your readers interested. When you review your notes, ask yourself the following questions: What's the headline here? What would be the first line of the article? What would each paragraph be about? (This is an excellent way to prepare for exams.)

The Need for Speed

When it comes to taking notes, every second counts. Even saving a fraction of a second here and there can make the difference between keeping up with the lecture and getting left in the dust. Here's how you can become a veritable speed demon in the classroom.

- **Never write in full sentences**. Leave out articles, adjectives, and adverbs, unless they add meaning to what's being discussed. The goal is to strip away all unnecessary parts of a sentence until only the skeleton remains. I call this "Neanderthal writing." When you read the notes back to yourself, you should sound like a caveman!
- **Access your inner thesaurus**. When your teacher uses long words, substitute shorter synonyms—for example, "but" instead of "however," "means" instead of "signifies," and "so" instead of "therefore."
- Use **arrows** to link a term or concept to points that are being made about it on different parts of the page. That way you can avoid having to rewrite it, and you've got a visual representation of the concept in your notes.

- **Neatness doesn't count.** I've seen people turn their notebooks into works of art—writing in perfectly straight lines, crossing every t and dotting every i, even using liquid paper in the middle of a lecture. But taking pride in one's penmanship isn't always a good thing. In the time they spent beautifying their notes, they may have missed a major point the teacher just made. It doesn't matter how you write, as long as *you* can read your chicken scratch.

- It's generally faster to write big than small—and paper is cheap—so go ahead and fill the page with a *gigantic scrawl.*

- Don't underestimate **the power of the pen**. I've had some pens that were so hard to write with, it felt like I was carving letters in stone. Note that a more expensive pen doesn't necessarily mean a faster pen. I've had plenty of 25-cent disposables that wrote better than a $250 ballpoint beauty. If you prefer pencils, go with the mechanical kind to avoid constant re-sharpening

- Unless your teacher is a very slow talker, **don't use colored pens or highlighters** while taking notes—it wastes precious time. Save such things for after class, when you can afford to spruce things up. However, if you have a lot of trouble paying attention in class, color-coding your notes may actually help you focus.

- If you had trouble writing down everything you wanted to, **review your notes immediately after class** while your memory is still fresh. This is a good time to add context, fill in gaps, and make things more legible.

In Their Own Words

"When taking notes, I try to use as many diagrams, arrows, etc., as possible. This prevents my notes from simply being a jumble of words, and makes them easier to follow."

—Top student at Columbia

Cursive is not a dirty word, though it's getting harder and harder to find in the classroom. Indiana's Department of Education, for example, has stopped requiring children to learn it.[54] The idea is that, in this computerized age, script handwriting is no longer a necessity—but this is doing our next generation of scholars a grave injustice. You can't always depend on a computer keyboard when you're taking notes or writing essays for an exam (more on this later), and printing your letters like a kindergartener just won't cut it.

A Brief Introduction to Shorthand

Shorthand is essential for fast, efficient note-taking. One common method is to use mathematical symbols to represent words and concepts. For example:

+	and, in addition to, plus
−	except for, excluding, minus
=	equals, is equal to, is the same as
≈	is similar to, is like, is about, resembles (You can shorten ≈ to ~, which is faster to write)
<	is/has less than
>	is/has more than, exceeds
∴	therefore, thus, because
→	leads to, results in, means, signifies
↑	gets bigger, increases, grows
↓	gets smaller, decreases, shrinks
Δ	change in [something]

You should also use abbreviations for common words, such as:

w/	with
w/o	without
w/in	within
b/c	because
b/w	between
accdg	according to
ex	for example
re:	regarding, pertaining to
vs	versus, as opposed to
c	century
diff	different
ppl	people

Develop your own abbreviations for different types of courses. I used "Xstian" for Christian in my history classes, "arch" for architecture in my art classes, "comp" for computer in my computer science classes, and, well, I think you get the idea. You can also take notes like you're texting your BFF. Write words the way they sound rather than how they're spelled—for example, "4eign" for "foreign," "l8r" for "later," and "cre8" for "create."

However, don't go overboard on the shorthand. You shouldn't abbreviate every word or devise a system of notation that's more complicated than the class itself. Keep in mind that you'll have to interpret these symbols later, which can be distracting and time-consuming when you're studying for an exam.

How to Tell What's Important

Taking notes shouldn't be a passive activity. You're not just recording things without thinking. You're keeping an ear out for the Big Ideas and distinguishing them from sub-points and supporting details.

This isn't always easy to do, as many teachers will go off on tangents and take a long time to get to the point, but the following tips will help you zero in on what's truly important—and what's more likely to show up on exams.

- **Listen for verbal cues**—such as *however, nevertheless, therefore, the point is, as we can see, in conclusion,* and *this leads us to conclude*—which indicate your teacher is about to make an important point. You should also include these keywords (or shorter synonyms) in your notes, to put things in context.
- **Copy down whatever the teacher writes on the board**, word for word. If they take the time to write it, it's probably important.
- **Teachers often start a lecture by saying what they're going to look at today.** Don't just take these statements for granted; write them down and underline them. When you're reviewing your notes for the exam weeks or months from now, the main topic of the lecture might not seem so obvious.
- If your teacher provides you with a **syllabus** at the beginning of the term, don't throw it into the bottomless pit of your backpack and never look at it again. **Review it before each class and when you're studying for exams.** Syllabi often provide useful information about the topics and structure of each day's lesson.
- It's not just about what your teacher says—it's also about **how** he or she says it. When your teacher speaks slowly and emphatically, it's probably important. They may also look meaningfully at the class, raise their eyebrows, or move their arms around—little gestures you would have to be in class to see.
- Always write down **factual details** such as names, places, dates, formulas, and so on.
- **A picture really is worth a thousand words** when it comes to

your notes. Make sure you copy every visual aid, graph, chart, and diagram your teacher shows you in class. These make complex concepts so much easier to understand. If you take an art history class, make quick sketches of paintings and objects so you can identify them later on exams.

- If the teacher goes over **how to do something**—like how to solve a math problem—write down every step in excruciating detail and make sure you understand it. There's a good chance you'll see a similar problem on the exam.

- Whenever your teacher **phrases something in the form of a question**, pay extra close attention. Write down the question (with a big Q next to it), the debate, and the answer (with a big A next to it), if there is one.

- If your teacher discusses the **causes of something**, it's probably important. Be sure to write down all the causes, preferably with numbers.

- If your teacher mentions **a passage or page in a book**, record all the information—title, author, page number—so you can look at it later.

- If one of your classmates (or you) makes a comment that the teacher **likes or agrees with, or both**, it's worth writing down.

- If your teacher shows a video or plays a recording in class, don't just use this as an opportunity to zone out—**include these multimedia experiences in your notes**. Teachers will often test you on them to see if you've been paying attention.

- **Make note of your uncertainties**, too. If you're not sure how to spell a word, write "sp?" next to it and get the correct spelling from Google or your textbook after class. If you don't understand something and there isn't time to ask questions, circle it and draw a big question mark in the margin. If you fall behind and miss part of the lecture, leave some room in your notes—you can ask your teacher or another good note-taker to fill in the missing info later.

- Sometimes a teacher will say in passing, "**You know, this would be a good test question.**" On those rare occasions, do not assume that he or she is joking or just making small talk. Instead, write down exactly what your teacher said, circle it, star it, and write "Test Question" next to it in big letters.

- **Teachers make important points at the end of class**. They may give their conclusions about something, announce an upcoming quiz, or give a clue about what's going to be on the exam. But all too often, your fellow classmates are packing up, zipping their book bags, scraping their chairs, and chattering to each other in their happiness at being let out of class. Don't be one of these people. It won't kill you to sit still for another minute or two. Unfortunately, your classmates' impatience can make it hard for you to hear these concluding remarks, so sit up front or go to the teacher after class for clarification.

How to Organize Your Notes

Good notes should separate the big ideas from the less-important-but-still-worth-knowing stuff while showing how they relate to each other. Here are some ways to add meaning to your notes.

- **Divide and conquer.** Always date your notes and draw lines across the page whenever your teacher starts a new topic. Leave some space after important points to make them stand out.

- **Indent for sub-points, causes, reasons, and examples,** and number them if you can. This makes it easier for your brain to process information than if your notes are in one big lump.

- Use **special symbols** to quickly add emphasis to your notes. Feel free to come up with your own notation, but I use underlines, circles, and stars to create a hierarchy of importance.

When I underline something, that means it's a vocab term or a new topic. I circle key points and draw stars to indicate potential test questions. Circling and starring something give it the highest importance. I use this for major clues about exams and potential paper topics.

- **The margins of your notebook** may seem like forbidden territory. You've always been taught to write inside the lines, right? Well, it's time to take advantage of this wasted space. The things you write here will really stand out, so save the space for things of über-high importance or things to follow up on—for example, terms to look up, questions to answer, ideas for paper topics, dates and deadlines, and information about exams.

How to Take Notes in a Seminar or Discussion Section

In classes such as seminars and discussion sections, the teacher's role is very different from what it is in a lecture—so how you take notes will have to change, too. In these classes, the teacher will usually provide a brief introduction and then guide the students into a lively discussion. (At least, that's the idea—some discussions are more dead than alive.) When your teacher speaks, you should take notes as you would during a lecture.

But once the class shifts into a student-led debate, it's time for a new strategy. You should focus on participating in the discussion, since that's the purpose of the class and it's probably what you're being graded on. For the most part, you're not going to be tested on what your classmates say. But if they mention something really interesting or thought-provoking, jot it down—it could come in handy for a paper topic later. You should also write down any comment your teacher singles out for extra attention.

Knowing how to take A+ notes is one thing, but knowing what to do with them is another. Once the information's in your notebook, don't just let it sit there until it's time to study for the exam. Reviewing your notes **within twenty-four hours** of when you took them will help keep you from forgetting the material. This is a good time to highlight key points and write down your thoughts and reactions. Some students find that rewriting or summarizing their notes after class makes the material really stick in their brains.

In Their Own Words

"A tip that makes studying easier [and] cuts down the amount of time is to type out your class notes later in the day after class. I always hand-wrote my notes and then typed them later.... [I]t was a quick review of what I had learned that day and it eliminated the hours spent before an exam trying to type a study sheet—I could just copy and paste from class notes....Typing out notes after handwriting them may seem like a waste of time, but I found that it really did not take long at all...plus it's a great review tool that helps you retain information."

—Student at NYU Law School

Sample Lecture and Notes

Let's take a look at these note-taking techniques in action. On pages 98 to 106, the left-hand column contains the transcript of a Yale lecture on Roman architecture taught by Professor Diana Kleiner;* the boxes on the right show my thought process as I turn her speech into notes. This is followed by my actual notes—use the numbers to match up the transcript and thoughts with the final product.

---

*Diana E. E. Kleiner, Roman Architecture (Yale University: Open Yale Courses), http://oyc.yale.edu, accessed August 27, 2011. License: Creative Commons BY-NC-SA.

Last time I introduced you to some of Rome's greatest buildings, and I remind you of two of them here: the Pantheon, on the left-hand side of the screen, the temple to all the gods, and then, of course, the Colosseum, on the right-hand side of the screen.

These are two of the greatest master-works of Roman architecture, and we will gain momentum and work our way up to those in the course of the semester, but it's not where we're going to begin. We're not going to begin with these masterworks; we're going to begin at the beginning. And the beginning goes way, way back, in fact all the way to the Iron Age, indeed to the eighth century BC.

And we know on precisely what day, not only the history of Rome but the history of Roman architecture began, and that was specifically on the twenty-first of April in 753 BC, because it was on the twenty-first of April in 753 BC that, according to legend, Romulus founded the city of Rome. Romulus founded the city of Rome on one of Rome's seven hills, the Palatine Hill.

① If she's reminding us of them, they must be important. It's always good to write down names, places, dates, and other keywords—they have a tendency to show up on tests. I'll save a few seconds by using a plus sign for "and," the number 2 instead of "two," and abbreviating the word "buildings". I'll put them in parentheses because they're just a reminder of what we did last time.

② Okay, she uses the word "beginning" a lot, so I'll underline it for emphasis. What better place to begin than the beginning? She also defined it with a key term (the Iron Age) and a time period.

③ She distinguishes between two major concepts here: the history of Rome and the history of Roman architecture. I'll connect them with a plus sign—this is much easier than writing "not only...but." She's saying they both began on a specific date, a detail that could be used as an exam question. And the major event that happened on that date is Romulus' founding of Rome on Palatine Hill. I'll note in parentheses that the Romulus story is a legend.

And I show you here a view of the Palatine Hill. This is taken from Google Earth.

I urged you last time to make sure that you have Google Earth downloaded on your computer and to take advantage of using Google Earth in the course of this semester in order to really get to know the city of Rome and the location of the various buildings that we'll be talking about within the city fabric.

So I show you one of these views of the Palatine Hill in Rome, from Google Earth, and you can see the relationship of that hill to the part of Rome in which it finds itself. You're going to be able to pick all of these buildings out by yourselves in the very near future, but let me just do that for you here this morning.

You can see, of course, the Colosseum, in the upper right corner. You can see the Roman Forum lying in front of it. You can see the great—that modern street that you see right behind the Forum is the Via dei Fori Imperiali, commissioned by Mussolini, Il Duce. We can also see in this view the Capitoline Hill with the oval piazza designed by Michelangelo, and down here the famous Circus Maximus, as you can see, the great stadium, the greatest stadium

④ I'll write down the abbreviation "img"—short for image—to remind myself that she's referring to a slide. I might want to look at it later when I'm studying for exams. Sometimes images are posted on class websites. If not, I can look it up on Google.

⑤ She's reminding us to use Google Earth, so it must be important. It shows that one of her priorities is for us to see the location of buildings in context. Google Earth will be a good resource when writing papers and reviewing for exams, so I'll put a starred note in the margin to remember to use it.

⑥ This is another hint that she will expect us to know these buildings visually and contextually; she might ask us to ID them on exams. I'll circle the note I just made in the margin.

⑦ She's giving us a lot of terms here, so I've got to write them down fast. These are probably things she'll expect us to know later in the semester. The Circus Maximus sounds particularly important. I'll indent and put them in parentheses since they're not our focus now.

of Rome. It wasn't the only stadium of Rome but it was the largest, and you can see its hairpin shape right down here.

The hill in question right now is the Palatine Hill, and this is the Palatine Hill, all of this area here.

And as you look down on it, as you gaze down on it, you will see the remains of a colossal structure, which is actually a late first-century AD palace that was designed under the direction of the emperor of Rome at that particular time, a very colorful character that we'll talk about in some detail later in the term, by the name of Domitian. This is Domitian's Palace on the Palatine Hill. But that discussion of that palace lies in the future.

What I want to say today is miraculously the remains of Romulus' village on the Palatine Hill, founded in the eighth century BC, actually lie beneath the remains of the Palace of Domitian in Rome, and it's to Romulus' huts on the Palatine Hill that I want to turn to today. Believe it or not, remains of those huts from the Iron Age are still there. Now they don't look like much. I'm showing you what remains of Romulus' huts right there, and you're probably having a hard time figuring out exactly what we're looking at.

(8) Okay, now she's looping back to her main subject, as I can tell from the phrase "in question right now."

(9) She's giving us the following information about the structure: its size, period, location, and name. I don't need to worry about the palace now, though, because she'll be coming back to it later. I'll put it in parentheses since it's a sidenote.

(10) Okay, I know she's coming to her main topic because it's what she "want[s] to say today." "Miraculously" is a pretty strong word, so I'll include that in my notes, but I'll write "miracle" instead of "miraculously" to save a second or two. I'll underline "the remains of Romulus' village" as her main topic. I'll also start abbreviating Romulus. Again, note the wording: "...that I want to turn to today." This is definitely her main topic. I'll circle this as it deserves more emphasis than an underline. The words "Believe it or not" reinforce how strongly she feels about the fact that they're still there. I can abbreviate Domitian with a 'D' because it's the only D word I've heard so far and won't get confused with something else. Lastly, I'll write "img" to remember that she's referring to a slide.

But what we're looking at—the architects that were working for the designers, that were working for Romulus, were very clever indeed, and they realized that the best way to create a foundation or a pavement for their huts was to use the natural rock of the Palatine Hill. And that's exactly what they did.

(11) I'll include the idea that there was a sort of chain of command from Romulus to the architects, and I'll include why she thinks they were clever. I can also substitute the words "saw" for "realized" and "make" for "created," and I'll start abbreviating Palatine as "Pal." Little things like this can save precious seconds.

What you're looking at here is the tufa, t-u-f-a, the natural tufa rock of the Palatine Hill.

(12) If she's spelling a word for us, it's worth writing down. I'll underline it as a key term.

And what they did was they created a rectangular plan. They gave it rounded corners, and they cut the stone back about twenty inches down to create that rectangular shape; they rounded the corners, and then they put holes in the tufa rock. The holes were to support wooden poles that served to support the superstructure of the hut and also to support the walls of the hut.

(13) Since she's talking about what the architects did, I'll draw an arrow from the first mention of the term "architects" to this line. This shows her train of thought and saves me from having to rewrite the word. I'll outline what she's telling us about the huts to make it easier to read. It's hard to think of shorter synonyms for the words "support" or "superstructure," so I'll just write them out.

So the pavement of the tufa rock of the Palatine is the floor of the hut, and then these holes support the wooden poles that supported, in turn, the superstructure.

(14) I just defined tufa, so I'll add this point to the definition. I already wrote down that the holes supported wooden poles that in turn supported the superstructure, so I don't need to say it again.

I now show you a restored view, on the left.

> (15) Again, I'll remind myself that she's referring to an image.

And you should all have your Monument Lists and should be able to follow along with the major monuments. You won't see every image that I'm going to be showing here, but you'll see a selection there of the ones that you'll need to learn and be able to talk about for the midterm, the two midterm exams in this course.

> (16) This is a major tip for the midterm exams: the images we need to know are on this list. I'll circle and star it in the margin so I'll be sure not to miss it.

But you'll see there this restored view of one of these Palatine huts, as well as a view of the model that one can actually see in the archaeological museum that's on the Palatine Hill today. You can see, as you look at this restored view on the left, you can see that rectangular plan that we talked about here; you can see the rounded corners, and you can see the wooden poles that were placed into those holes to support the walls and the superstructure of the building. You can see over here the same, the wooden poles. This gives you a better sense of what they looked like in actuality, the wooden poles and also the superstructure.

> (17) The restored view and the model show the features I noted earlier. I'll draw an arrow to indicate this.

We also know what the walls were made out of. They were made out of something—and I put some of the keywords that might be unfamiliar to you on the Monument List as well—they were made out of wattle and daub. Well, what is wattle and daub? Wattle and daub is twigs and rods that are covered and plastered with clay; twigs and rods covered and plastered with clay. That served as the walls of the structure, and then the sloping roof, as you see it here, was thatched.

Now it's very hard—there are no huts that look like this in Rome still today that I can show you to give you a better sense of what these would've looked like in antiquity.

But I'm sure you, like I, have seen huts like this on your travels around the world. And one example I can show you—and would that we were all down there right now. This is a view of a small village in the Maya Riviera, near Cancun, where one sees, if you take the bus or a car from Maya to Chichen Itza, which I hope some of you have had a chance to do. If you haven't, it's a great trip. And you can see all along the road huts that look very much like the huts of Romulus' village, made out of wood and then with thatched roofs, as you can see here. So this is the best I can do in terms of conjuring up for you Romulus' village.

(18) She's defining a term that's on the Monument List, so there's a good chance it'll show up on an exam. I'll underline it and use an equal sign for definition. The words "covered" and "plastered" mean basically the same thing, so I'll only write one of them.

(19) This is worth noting, if only because it shows her train of thought.

(20) The stuff about us traveling around the world is extraneous, but buried in this anecdote is an important point: the ancient huts resemble ones in Mexico. I'll use a "~" symbol to indicate similarity.

We also have information with regard to what these huts looked like in ancient Roman times or—not in ancient Roman, in the Iron Age, as I mentioned before. We have not only the pavement stone that's still preserved, but we also have these urns. We call them hut urns, hut urns, because they're urns in the shape of huts.

And these hut urns were used for cremation, in the eighth century BC— these date also to the Iron Age—and the cremated remains of the individual were placed inside the door of the hut.

And if you look at this hut urn, you'll see that it looks very similar to the huts of Romulus that we've already been talking about. It is either sort of square or rectangular in shape. It has rounded corners, as you can see here, and the roof of the hut urn is sloping.

So we do believe we use this, along with the surviving pavement, to restore what these huts of Romulus looked like in the eighth century BC.

21 She's telling us about another kind of evidence used to reconstruct the huts—these things called hut urns, which I'll underline as a key term. Note that I started writing the purpose of hut urns (i.e. another source of information about what the huts looked like) before she said what they're called—otherwise I wouldn't have time to write everything down.

22 There are two things worth noting here: the hut urns' function and date. I'll add them to the line I just wrote.

23 She's referring to the same features I wrote down earlier, so I won't rewrite them. The main point here is that the hut urns look like Romulus' huts.

24 She already said this, so I'm not going to write it again

Let me also note—it's interesting just to see the status of men and women in any given civilization at any given time.

There are essentially two kinds of hut urns from the eighth century BC. Excuse me, there are two kinds of urns in the eighth century BC. One of them is hut urns and the other is helmet urns, and you can guess, as well as anyone, as to who was buried in which. The men were buried in the helmet urns and the women's remains were placed in the hut urns. So men's domain was considered the battlefield; women's domain was considered the house.

But the houses are actually more important in terms of giving us a sense again of what Romulus' village looked like in the eighth century.

And if you take one of those huts and you combine it with another set of huts, you can get a sense of what the village of Romulus would have looked like in the eighth century BC.

25 She's kind of going off on a tangent here, as I can tell from the words "Let me also note," so I'll indent this point. Since she says it's interesting, I'll underline it.

26 She's introducing a lot of new concepts here, so to keep up I have to write with as little waste as possible. I'll include the two types of urns, with a parentheses next to each one to indicate the gender. This way I'm only writing "hut" and "helmet urns" once. I can use an arrow to indicate that the type of urn leads us to conclude the domains of men and women, and an equals sign to define what these are.

27 I can use a greater-than sign to show that hut urns, or houses, are "more important" than helmet urns.

28 I'll use a right arrow here to indicate that combining hut urns can lead to a sense of what an actual village would have looked like.

This is a model that is on view in the archaeological museum on the Palatine Hill today, and it gives you a very good sense of the village of Romulus in the eighth century.

And of course it was from this village that the great city of Rome grew, and of course there's a quite significant difference between Rome as it is now and Rome as it was in the eighth century BC.

(29) Again, I'll note that she's talking about an image to remind myself to look at it when I'm studying.

(30) The fact that Rome grew from this village gives a sense of closure to this topic. The statement that there's "a quite significant difference" between Rome then and now is so obvious that I'm not going to include it. I'll use an arrow to represent the idea of growth.

1/15

Romulus Founds Rome

(Pantheon + Colosseum – 2 of Rome's greatest bldgs) ①

Beginning – Iron Age, 8th c. BC ②

History of Rome + Roman arch. began 4/21/753 – Romulus

founds Rome on Palatine Hill (legend) ③

*Use Google ⑥
Earth for Rome
 – location of ⑤
bldgs w'in city

img – Palatine Hill on Google Earth ④

(Colosseum,

Roman Forum,

Via dei Fori Imperiali – modern, Mussolini,

Capitoline Hill – oval piazza, Michelangelo,

Circus Maximus – largest stadium in Rome) ⑦

(Huge structure, late 1st c. AD, Palatine – Domitian's palace) ⑨

Miracle – (Remains of Rom.'s village) founded 8th c. BC on

Palatine, beneath D's Palace – still there! (img) ⑩

Architects, worked for designers, worked for Rom.

  clever – saw best way to make foundation/ pavement was to

use Pal Rock ⑪

Tufa – rock of Pal. = floor of hut ⑭
    ⑫

  – rectangular plan

- rounded corners

- cut stone 20 in. down

- put holes in tufa to support wood poles for superstructure + walls [13]

*Monument
List – know [16]
for 2 mdtms

img – restored view [15] + model of Pal. huts [17]

Walls of <u>wattle</u> + <u>daub</u> = twigs, rods covered w/ clay

Sloping roof – thatched [18]

No huts like this in Rome now. [19]

img – village in Mexico

Rom.'s huts ~ huts in Maya Riviera near Cancun [20]

Other source re what huts looked like besides pavement stone –

in shape of huts = <u>Hut urns</u> [21] – cremation, 8th c. BC [22] ~ Rom.'s huts [23]

<u>Status of men + women</u> [25]

2 kinds of urns – hut (female) + helmet (male) urns →

- men's domain = battlefield

- women's = house [26]

Hut urns > helmet urns at giving sense of Rom.'s village [27]

Combining hut urns → sense of what village looked like [28]

(img – Model at arch. museum on Pal) [29]

village → Rome [30]

If I had to write a headline based on my notes, it would be, "Remains of Romulus' village discovered on the Palatine!" The first line would read, "Archaeologists have discovered the remains of what appears to be an eighth-century BC settlement on the Palatine Hill in Rome." The first paragraph would give a detailed description of the huts; the second would explain how archaeologists are reconstructing what these huts looked like.

Seven Common Excuses for Taking Bad Notes (and Why They're Wrong)

We saw in the last section how you can condense ten minutes of lecture into two pages of notes that effectively capture the professor's arguments, supporting details, and train of thought. This isn't very hard to do—and yet many people don't even try to do it, as I could tell by borrowing their notes and looking around the room during class. I often wondered why so many students sat there like lumps, barely moving their pens over the page, passively listening to what the teacher was saying—if they were listening at all. Let's take a look at some common reasons for taking bad notes. Do any of these sound familiar to you?

Excuse 1: I'll Remember the Lecture Better if I Just Sit Back and Listen.

Unless you've got a photographic memory, this is what's known as a *bad idea*. According to a study by John McLeish, students remember only 42 percent of what their teacher said by the time class ends, and about 20 percent a week later.[55] Did you catch that last part? Twenty percent! And that number will be even smaller when you sit down to take the test—if you don't have good notes to refresh your memory, that is. Research also shows that students recall more of the lecture if they record it in their notes.[56]

Excuse 2: Everything I Need to Know Is in My Textbook, So It Doesn't Matter if I Take Notes.

There are at least two things wrong with this statement. First of all, most teachers talk about and test you on more than what's in the textbook, so unless these things are in your notes, you probably won't see them again until the day of the exam. And second, good notes can make reading the textbook faster and more productive—or even unnecessary!

Excuse 3: I Can't Write Fast Enough, So What's the Point?

Sometimes students are so overwhelmed by the pace of a class that they throw their pens down in defeat, but this doesn't have to happen! There are plenty of things you can do to take control of the situation. For example:

- **Know your notes**. Analyze them after class or at the end of each day. Ask yourself the following questions:
    - Am I trying to record too much?
    - Am I using abbreviations, simplified sentence structure, arrows, and other techniques to speed up my writing?
    - Am I trying to be too neat?
    - Is my pen easy to write with?

    Practice rewriting your notes in a more efficient format, using the techniques we discussed earlier.
- **Get back on track.** If you find yourself still writing something the teacher discussed five minutes ago, don't panic! Leave some space in your notes and ask your teacher or a conscientious classmate to help fill in the missing links after class.
- **Practice makes perfect.** Try out your techniques on news shows, documentaries, and lessons on TV or the Internet.

Build up your endurance like a runner: start off with short, five-minute sprints and work your way up to two-hour note-taking marathons.

- If your teacher is a certifiable motor mouth, it's okay to ask him or her—politely, of course—to **slow down**. Speak to your teacher after class or during office hours about your concerns. Most teachers aren't aware that they're going too fast and will appreciate your honesty.

- If you can't write fast enough no matter how hard you try, or if your handwriting is illegible, a **keyboard may be the answer**. (See page 114 for tips on using computers in the classroom.)

- You should only **tape-record lectures as a last resort**. If you're not careful, you'll end up spending twice as much time in class as you bargained for. However, tape recording may be a good option for aural learners—that is, people who learn best by listening. In this case, replaying the lecture may be more beneficial than reading your notes.

Excuse 4: I Only Need to Write Down What the Teacher Puts on the Board.

You should include everything your teacher writes down word for word, but don't stop there! Copying what's on the board may have sufficed in elementary school, but in high school and college this is usually the bare minimum of what you have to know.

Excuse 5: My Class Has Slides that I Can Access Online, So I Don't Need to Take Notes.

PowerPoint presentations aren't just for the boardroom anymore. It's common nowadays for teachers to use slides in their lectures and post them online. Although this would seem to make students' lives easier, it can lull you into a false sense of security if you're not careful. A lot of people simply sit back and stop taking notes, thinking that everything they need to know is on the slides. But most decks are spotty, incomplete, and confusing. They may be sufficient for business meetings, but not for studying for exams.

That doesn't mean you should ignore them, though. Slides can make taking notes easier, faster, and more accurate, if used the right way. The teacher's already given you most of the main points—you just have to fill in the detail. Here are some ways to do it.

Option 1: The Low-Tech Print Option

1. Prep time: if the slides are posted before class, print them out and number each one if they're not already numbered.
2. Bring the printouts and a notebook or binder to class.
3. Write today's date on your slides and in your notebook or binder.
4. Take notes directly on the slide printouts as they are covered in class. Flesh out the slide's outlines with details, examples, and so on.
5. If you run out of space on a slide, write that slide's number in your notebook and continue taking notes there. That way, your notes won't be limited by the size of the printout—and when you're reviewing, you can easily match up the slide with the relevant section in your notebook.
6. Make sure to staple the printouts and store them in a folder, or hole-punch them if you use a binder, so they won't get lost or out of order.

Option 2: The High-Tech No-Print Option

If you bring your computer to class and the slide deck is editable—it's a PowerPoint or Word document and not a pdf—you can save the file and type your notes directly on the slides. This avoids the confusion of having to go back and forth between the printouts and your notes. (However, bringing your laptop to class has its own set of drawbacks—more on this later.)

Option 3: The Low-Tech No-Print Option

If the slides are posted after class—or if you can't or don't want to print them out—take notes as you normally would. As each slide is discussed, write down that slide's number or, if you don't know it, the first few words of the slide in your notes, so you can match them up when you're reviewing.

Excuse 6: What My Teacher Says Is So Obvious, I Don't Need to Write It Down.

Were you ever in a situation where you felt like you could teach the class yourself? Well, maybe you could, but think twice before you start daydreaming or surreptitiously checking your iPhone. Something may sound obvious when you hear it, but that doesn't mean you'll remember it when test time rolls around, especially if you have to recall it for a long answer or essay question. Taking notes during a boring lecture will also help you stay focused—or at least keep you from falling asleep!

Excuse 7: My Classmates Aren't Taking Notes, So Why Should I?

Sure, it can feel weird to be the only one writing. You may think that if no one else is doing it, it can't be that important, right? But this is just a subtle form of peer pressure. Most people take far fewer notes than they should. According to one study, students fail to record 40 percent of important points during lectures.[57] So tune out what your friends are doing and get that pen moving!

Technology in the Classroom: Why Ditching Your Laptop May Be Good for Your Grades

You can type faster than you can write, so it makes sense for you to take notes on your computer, right? That's what lots of students have decided. But before you start lugging your laptop to class, there are some things you should consider.

First off, ask yourself the following question: Do you have enough self-control to use your laptop responsibly? Be honest, now. Most students who bring electronic devices into the classroom use them for extracurricular activities. In a 2006 study by Carrie Fried of Winona State University, people who brought computers to class admitted to spending nearly a quarter of the time using them for things besides taking notes—for example, checking email, IMing, surfing the Web, and playing games.[58]

But is this really a bad thing? Maybe today's students are so good at multitasking that they can still pay attention while doing all these activities. Sorry to burst your bubble, but the latest research suggests just the opposite. In a 2009 Stanford University study by Eyal Ophir, Clifford Nass, and Anthony Wagner, test subjects were separated into two groups: those who do a lot of media multitasking and those who do not. Experiments showed that the high multitaskers were worse at blocking out distractions, organizing and storing information, and switching from one task to another—all the things you'd think they'd be good at.[59]

"They're suckers for irrelevancy," said Clifford Nass, one of the researchers. "Everything distracts them."[60] The Winona State study also found that students who bring laptops to class don't learn as much and find lectures more confusing than their tech-free peers. The more they used their computers, the lower their classroom performance.[61]

In Their Own Words

"I would suggest avoiding taking notes on laptops or other electronic devices [like] smartphones [or] tablets. Although [the notes] are more legible, I find them to be less spontaneous and more difficult to organize."

—Top student at Columbia

"Not using my laptop during class eliminated [the] temptation to check email, Facebook, etc."

—Student at NYU Law School

Laptops aren't the only attention-grabbers in the classroom. According to a study by Deborah Tindell and Robert Bohlander at Wilkes University, more than 90 percent of college students have sent texts during lectures.[62] Unless you're expecting a really important call, do yourself and your teacher a favor and turn off your phone. Whatever it is can wait until the bell rings.

Of course, not everyone is multitasking when they bring their computers to class. Some people actually do take diligent notes. But even if you belong to this latter group, you should still think twice before you toss that notebook and pen. Researchers Anne Mangen and Jean-Luc Velay have found that writing by hand activates different parts of the brain than typing.[63] The motor actions and the sensation of holding a pen or pencil may actually aid in the learning process, forging a connection between what's on the paper and what's in your head. Plus, handwriting forces you to slow down and think about what you're writing, while typing makes it easy to zone out.

In Their Own Words

"I write things down by hand while I listen to or read them. After that point it's pretty much ingrained in my memory."

—Winner of the Google Anita Borg Memorial Scholarship

If You Must Type...

Some students just can't write fast enough to keep up with the teacher. Others have handwriting that resembles cuneiform. If, after trying all the techniques mentioned on the previous pages, your notes are still a hopeless mess, it *may* be time to start typing. If you do bring a PC to class, however, be smart about how you use it.

For starters, *don't transcribe the lecture word for word* just because you can. You should still use the techniques discussed above— abbreviations, simplified sentence structure, symbols, indentation, and so on. It's easier to review your notes this way than if they sound like a monologue, and it forces you to think about what you're writing. Similarly, don't have a field day with formatting and fonts—this wastes time and breaks concentration. Limit yourself to the big three: **bold**, underline, and *italic*.

Keep some loose-leaf paper handy in case you have to draw something or copy a diagram that would take too long to replicate on the computer. And last but certainly not least, *resist the urge to go online* while you're in class. If you need some help fighting temptation, disable your Wi-Fi or use an app—such as Freedom, Anti-Social, or Cold Turkey—that blocks your access to the Web or social networks.

Classroom netiquette. If you think that surfing the Web in the middle of a lecture isn't bothering anyone, think again. In the Winona State study, students rated their classmates' computer use as the single biggest distraction in the classroom—more than their own computer use, other students talking or fidgeting, the time of day, and the classroom environment.[64] Besides, do you really want everyone sitting behind you to see that embarrassing picture your ex posted of you on Facebook?

Exercises

Exercise 1:

This exercise is designed to help you put your new note-taking skills into practice.

Step 1: Take notes on a news show, documentary, or online lecture for three weeks using the techniques described in this chapter. In the first week, take notes for about five minutes a day. For the second week, increase it to fifteen minutes. In the third week, take notes continuously for thirty minutes a day.

Tip: Don't pause the show or lecture while you're taking notes; practice keeping up with the speaker in real time.

Step 2: After each session, review your notes and pretend you're using them to write an article. Answer the following questions on a separate piece of paper. (This is a great way to reinforce what you just learned and to make sure you're taking comprehensive notes.)

    a. What would the headline be?

    b. What would the first line of the article be?

    c. What would each paragraph be about?

Exercise 2:

Rewrite the notes from one of your classes using the techniques described in this chapter. Do this for about ten minutes every day for a week. Pay attention to your use of shorthand, simplified sentence structure, indentation, and so on. Ask yourself if it's clear what the big ideas and sub-points are. Then answer the following question:

What are three things you want to improve about the way you currently take notes? (Some examples would be making more use of abbreviations, including more information, and grouping together related ideas.)

1. _____

   _____

2. _____

   _____

3. _____

   _____

CHAPTER 6
Learning to Read (Again)

IN MY FRESHMAN AND sophomore years of college, I read dozens of books by the great thinkers of Western civilization. From Plato to Nietzsche, Homer to Shakespeare—you name it, I read it. At times it drove me crazy—picture reading hundreds of pages that sound like *this* every week: "All rational knowledge is either material and concerned with some object, or formal and concerned only with the form of understanding and of reason themselves and with the universal rules of thought in general without regard to differences of its objects." Come again, Kant?

Nevertheless, these classes were the most meaningful and rewarding of my entire academic career. I learned new ways of thinking and gained a deeper appreciation for the culture I live in. Perhaps just as importantly, I learned how to think about what I read. This is one of the most important parts of a well-rounded education, but it's a skill that many students fail to learn.

How to Be an Active Reader

Whether you're faced with a biology textbook or Immanuel Kant's *Critique of Pure Reason*, there are certain steps you should follow to get the most out of your reading. The first step is to engage in a little prereading warm-up. When you're given an assignment, don't just dive into it blindly—start by getting a sense of what the piece is about. Prep your brain by looking at things like headings, subheadings, captions, diagrams, introductions, conclusions, and end-of-chapter summaries. (Don't worry about giving away the ending.) If your teacher gave you questions about the reading, review them now so you can keep an eye out for the answers. Think of it as looking at a map to orient yourself in a new city.

One popular prereading technique is to *turn headings into questions*. For example, a section in your astronomy textbook called "The Origins of the Universe" would become "What are the origins of the universe?" Like a reporter, you're looking for the who, what, where, why, and when of every story. Do this for every heading or subheading in the assigned reading, and write them on a piece of paper. Preparing questions will give you a sense of what's to come; and when you start reading, it'll help you stay focused since you're looking for answers instead of giving every word equal weight. These questions also make excellent study aids, so keep them in a safe place until it's time to review.

In Their Own Words

"When assigned to read a lengthy article, essay, [or] scholarly work, try to use electronic databases like JSTOR, ProQuest, [and Lexis]Nexis to see if somebody has written a commentary or a critique of this particular piece. Often by reading a three-page critique (or two) you will be able to learn over 70 percent of what the work you have been assigned is about and save yourself a lot of time."

—Top student at Columbia

In-Depth Reading

When you read for fun, you probably go from beginning to end without pausing, writing, or questioning what the author says. This is exactly what you should *not* do when reading for school. As with studying, it pays to be active rather than passive. Interacting with the book will help you get more out of it. Treat it like a person you're having a conversation with—ask questions, make it repeat things, challenge it, talk back to it. The discussion may be one-sided, but it'll make you more aware of what you're reading.

When you come across a particularly difficult line or passage, *stop and say it in your own words*. If you get stuck, go over the part that's giving you trouble. (It often helps to read out loud.) When the author describes an event or process, visualize it in your head.

> **It's easy to be a speed reader!** Just move your finger (or a pencil) from left to right as you read each line. Your eye will instinctively follow along, keeping you fast and focused. There are lots more advanced speed-reading techniques out there, but this is one you can do without any practice—and it really works!

Taking Notes: The Key to Reading Success

One of the most powerful techniques for active reading is taking notes. Your notes are brief reminders of what you're reading *and* what you're thinking as you read. They should be much simpler and sparser than your lecture notes—each one no more than a couple of words or phrases—since you can always look at the text for clarification. The goal is to summarize anything that's important: big ideas, sub-points, arguments, causes, explanations, and so on. If you're reading something with a plot, you should also make note of key events. Last but not least, include your own thoughts and reactions to the text. (More on this later.)

Keep It Simple

If you come across a paragraph or page where nearly everything seems important, don't go crazy taking notes. Just put a star next to it, draw a bracket from the beginning to the end of the important text, and add a word or two on what it's about. It's better to reread the original than make notes that are as long as the text itself. If it's something you'll want to refer to a lot, write a few words on the edge of a Post-it note explaining what it is, and leave this note sticking out so you can see it. You'll be able to find and flip to what you need in seconds.

Reading with a Critical Eye

One of the most important things I learned to do in school was to challenge authority—or at least, authority in the form of books and articles. Although this isn't so important for textbooks, it's crucial when reading works of literature, political and philosophical treatises, persuasive essays, and much, much more. As you're reading, ask yourself questions like:

- Do you agree or disagree with what the author's saying, and why?
- Why is the author writing this? What are some possible motives or biases? What were the conditions (historical, socioeconomic, political) under which the author was writing?
- How does this point support the author's argument? Are there weaknesses or flaws in the argument?
- What assumptions does the author make? What does he or she take for granted?
- What are the broader implications of the author's argument?
- How does the author use language to affect, persuade, or manipulate the reader?
- How does this book compare to others you've read for this class?

- How does it compare to what's been discussed in class? Does it exemplify or break away from certain themes you've seen throughout the term?
- How could what the author's saying be applied to the present day?

Your answers to these questions should become part of your notes. If you find a hole in the author's argument, note this next to the relevant text. If a passage reminds you of something else you read, write down "similar to [fill in the blank]." If you think that what someone wrote hundreds or thousands of years ago could be applied to contemporary society, write that down, too. Your thoughts are valuable; they deserve a place next to the printed word.

Notes. What Are They Good For?

So what's the point of taking notes when you have the text right in front of you? Three words: reinforcement, review, and reference.

1. **Reinforcement**: Have you ever spent hours poring over an extremely dense, complicated text, only to reach the end and realize you have no idea what you just read? Well, notes can help prevent this embarrassing situation. Taking them forces you to think about what you're reading, while going over them helps you remember it.

2. **Review**: Look over your notes before classes where you have to discuss the reading so you can remember what you want to say. During exam time, instead of rereading the whole book or searching for the important bits, you can glance at your notes to quickly refresh your memory. Your notes can also indicate which passages deserve a second, or third, or fourth look before a test.

3. **Reference**: If you have to discuss the readings in class or for

a paper, let your notes be your guide. Let's say your teacher tells you to turn to page 65 and discuss the meaning of the "noble savage" in Rousseau's *Discourse on the Origin of Inequality.* So you turn to that page and instead of having to reread some of the densest language you've ever seen, your notes remind you straight away that the noble savage exists between nature and civilization and is the happiest state of man. *Boom!* Your hand shoots up while the rest of your classmates are still trying to skim the impenetrable text.

> **Here's a couplet for you:** The denser the book, the less you'll retain. Reading your notes makes it stick in your brain.

Where Should Your Notes Go?

If you own the book, you should *write your notes in the margins* rather than on loose-leaf paper or the computer. You don't want to keep moving your eyes, hands, and attention from one place to another; writing in the book helps minimize these costly breaks in concentration. It's also easier to refer back to the original text if your notes are right next to it. In most cases, you're going to be sitting in class with the book in front of you, discussing specific passages. Having everything in one place makes it easier to follow along and participate.

If you don't own the book or the margins aren't wide enough, *write your notes on Post-its* and stick them next to the relevant text. Or you can photocopy the readings and mark them up however you like. If you do write your notes on a separate piece of paper, though, be sure to include the title and page numbers for easy reference.

In addition to writing in the margin, you should also *mark up the text as you read.* Circle or underline definitions, key terms, and words that signify a point is being made—such as "however," "nevertheless," "moreover," "in addition," "more importantly," "thus," "therefore," "as we can see," and "because." This helps you slow down when you're reading important passages and makes it easier to locate them when you're reviewing.

If the author is listing things such as causes, arguments, examples, or ideas, *number each item* to make it easier to keep track. You should also put question marks next to sections you don't understand. When you're finished with the reading, see if these parts are any clearer. If not, write down your questions on a piece of paper and ask your teacher or TA about them later.

If you're reading a scholarly article—one that comes from an academic journal—keep an eye out for the thesis (the main argument of the piece). This isn't always easy to spot, as most academics don't conveniently put it at the end of the intro. Usually the first few paragraphs will build up to it. When you *do* find the thesis, circle or underline the whole thing and make sure you can explain it in your own words. As you read through the article, number each point supporting the thesis to make them stand out.

Second time's the charm. If the reading is short enough—for example, an article or a chapter in a book—it's often helpful to read it twice. The first time, go through it quickly without pausing to make notes or ask questions. It's okay if you don't understand something at this point—just keep going. When you read it the second time—preferably after a day or two have gone by—use the active reading techniques described above. Giving the material time to sink into your brain can make the second pass much more rewarding. In classes where you have hundreds of pages of reading per week, however, rereading isn't very realistic. You'll typically have time for only one read-through, so you've got to make it count.

The final part of the reading process is to do something with what you've read—summarize it, draw conclusions, ask questions, apply the formulas you learned, and so on. Your teacher will usually supply you with an exercise asking you to do just that. But if not, take some time to reflect on the reading. Make a three- or four-line summary, and write down any thoughts or questions you have about the text as a whole. Ask yourself what the author's main idea is. For a math or science book, do a few practice problems on what you just read. If you made questions out of the headings back in the prereading stage, now's the time to make sure you can answer them.

Sample Text with Notes

Let's take a look at this paragraph from John Stuart Mill's *On Liberty*. This text is so dense that it can go in one eye and out the other, but taking notes will help it stay in your head. I've included my thought process in italics, as well as some questions you could ask yourself while you're reading. My sample notes are in the margins.

Liberty vs. Authority

The <u>struggle between Liberty and Authority</u> is the most con-

Mill's Background?

spicuous feature in the portions of history with which we are earliest familiar, particularly in that of (Greece) (Rome) and (England).

There are a few clues that the "struggle between Liberty and Authority" is the main topic here: it's in the beginning of the paragraph, Mill calls it the "most conspicuous feature," and the first letter of each term is capitalized. I'll underline it and write it in the margin. I'm not sure why he lumps England together with Greece and Rome, so I'll circle those terms for now. As soon as someone starts throwing around terms such as "struggle," "liberty," and "authority," I want to know their background and the socioeconomic conditions under which they were writing. I'll write a note to myself in the margin to look that up.

In old times.

But in (old times) this contest was between <u>subjects,</u> or some

struggle = subject vs. government

classes of subjects, <u>and the government</u>. By <u>liberty</u>, was meant <u>protection against the tyranny of the political rulers</u>. The rulers were conceived (except in some of the popular governments of Greece) as in a necessarily antagonistic position to the people whom they ruled.

liberty = protection from tyranny

> *Mill's defining what struggle and liberty were "in old times" —but exactly what times were these? I'll put a question mark here. Definitions are important, so I'll summarize them in the margins.*
>
> *Questions you might ask yourself:*
>
> > *1. What are these "old times" that Mills speaks of? Prehistory? Antiquity? The Middle Ages?*
> >
> > *2. What is the significance of liberty being protection from tyranny? How does this compare with the present-day definition of liberty?*

They consisted of a governing One, or a governing tribe or caste, who derived their authority from inheritance or conquest; who, at all events, did not hold it at the pleasure of the governed, and whose supremacy men did not venture, perhaps did not desire, to contest, whatever precautions might be taken against its oppressive exercise. Their power was regarded as <u>necessary, but also as highly dangerous</u>; as a <u>weapon</u> which they would attempt to use against their subjects, no less than against external enemies.

Ruler's power was necessary BUT dangerous

> *These lines boil down to the following: the ruler's power in these "old times" was necessary but dangerous. I'll write this in the margins. I'm also wondering why this power was necessary at all— maybe he'll explain.*
>
> *Questions you might ask yourself:*
>
> > *1. How does Mill's view of the formation of government compare to that of other writers you may have read—such as Hume, Locke, Rousseau, etc.?*

To prevent the weaker members of the community from being

preyed upon by innumerable vultures, it was needful that there
should be an animal of prey stronger than the rest, commissioned to keep them down. But as the king of the vultures would
be no less bent upon preying upon the flock than any of the
minor harpies, it was indispensable to be in a perpetual attitude
of defense against his beak and claws. The aim, therefore, of
patriots, was to set limits to the power which the ruler should
be suffered to exercise over the community; and this limitation
was what they meant by liberty.

*He does explain why the ruler's power was necessary: to protect
the "weaker members of the community" from others who might
take advantage of them. But the people needed protection from the
ruler as well. Mill defines liberty here, but since it's basically the
same as what he said before (liberty = protection from tyranny), I
won't write it again.*

It was attempted in two ways. First, by obtaining a recognition
of certain immunities, called political liberties or rights, which it
was to be regarded as a breach of duty in the ruler to infringe, and
which, if he did infringe, specific resistance, or general rebellion,
was held to be justifiable. A second, and generally a later expedi-
ent, was the establishment of constitutional checks; by which the
consent of the community, or of a body of some sort supposed to
represent its interests, was made a necessary condition to some of
the more important acts of the governing power.

*Liberty achieved
in 2 ways: 1)
recognition of
political
liberties/rights
(else rebellion);
2) constitutional
checks —
consent for acts*

*Since Mill states that this limitation of power was achieved in two
ways, I know I have to be on the lookout for what these two things
are. Luckily he doesn't keep us waiting long. The ways of achieving
liberty seem pretty important, so I'll summarize them in the margins.*

Questions you might ask yourself:

*1. What are some examples of political liberties and constitu-
tional checks? What's the difference between them?*

*2. Do you agree with Mill's assessment of the two ways lib-
erty was achieved? Are there other ways besides these?*
*At the end of this section, I'm expecting Mill to discuss how the defi-
nition of liberty changed over time.*

Digital Books: Not Quite Ready for School?

Ebooks may be fine for reading a novel on the beach, but they've got
a long way to go when it comes to the classroom. The best readers
physically interact with their books—writing in the margins, circling
key passages, dog-earing pages, slapping on Post-it notes, picking up
other books for comparison, and so on. According to recent studies,
devices such as ebook readers and iPads don't yet have the flexibility
to accommodate these advanced reading techniques.

In 2009, a number of schools including Reed College, the
University of Washington, and Princeton University gave students
the Amazon Kindle DX to use in their classes. Although Reed students and faculty felt the device had a lot of potential, most reported
that it couldn't take the place of regular books due to issues with pdf
formatting, page refresh rate, the inability to display multiple texts,
and difficulties with highlighting and annotation.[65] University of
Washington researchers noted that the Kindle also disrupted cognitive mapping, a technique in which readers use the physical location
of the text to recall where they read it and retain information.[66]

While recent studies of the iPad in academia have been more favor-
able, there are still plenty of drawbacks. Students said the device helped
them feel connected and made learning more interesting, but a focus
group at the University of Notre Dame reported the following problems:

- Annotated highlighting leaves much to be desired.
- Typing or hand-writing notes on the device is difficult.
- Since windows cannot be opened side by side, it's hard to
  multitask.

- It's a pain to flip back and forth between pages of a book.
- The screen creates glare.[67]

So for serious reading, you may want to skip the technology and stick with the real thing for now.

> **A note about usability.** Although reading speeds on electronic devices are improving, they still haven't caught up to the printed page. In a study conducted by usability expert Jakob Nielsen, reading speeds on the iPad and Kindle were 6.2 percent and 10.7 percent slower, respectively, than reading the old-fashioned way.[68] And don't even think about doing serious studying on your iPhone—reading comprehension on this tiny screen is less than half what it is on a full-sized monitor.[69]

When to Read: The Before or After Debate

In addition to knowing *how* to read, you've also got to think about *when* to read. Your goal as a student should be to get the most out of your reading in the shortest time possible. A lot of people (your teachers included) will tell you to always do the readings before class. But the truth of the matter is, if you follow their advice, you may not have time for much else—homework, papers, extracurriculars, or sleep.

That's why you must plan your readings wisely. Think about what you'll be doing with this information. Will you need it for class, or can it wait until after you've heard the teacher discuss it? In situations like the following, you should do the readings *before* the bell rings:

- **If you're expected to answer questions about or discuss the readings in class.** This is particularly true of seminars and discussion sections, but some lectures will require participation, too. You'd better come prepared when your teacher is evaluating you based on what you say. Even here, though, be selective about what you read. If you have multiple textbooks, does your teacher focus on one more than the other(s)? Are some texts required while others are optional? Did your teacher ask questions that focus on specific parts of the reading?

- **If your teacher may give you a pop quiz on the reading.** Some teachers warn you in the beginning of the term that they'll do this dastardly deed; others don't. You should do the readings before class until you know where your teacher falls on the pop-quiz meter.

- **If the readings are short and provide good background for the lecture.** Case in point: the PowerPoint presentations many teachers post online before class.

- **If you're taking a lab.** Always read the instructions before setting foot in the laboratory. You'll need all the time you can get to perform your experiments.

- **If you know the teacher is going to discuss something really specific**—like a case study, a math problem, or a passage from a text. Review it before class.

In most other situations, however, it's better to attend class *first* and do the readings *second*. There are two major reasons for this.

- **Reading something after it's been discussed in class makes it easier to digest**. Think of it this way: the amount of time you spend in class is fixed, but the number of hours you spend reading is variable. If your teacher explains something well enough in class, you'll be able to get through the readings much faster than you would have without this introduction—or you may not have to do them at all!

- I'll let you in on a little secret: in most classes, you don't have to read everything. **By waiting until the teacher gives you hints about which parts are important, you can make an informed decision about what to read.** Cut down your study time by paying extra attention to the passages or chapters that were discussed in class, and skimming or skipping those that weren't.

> **IMPORTANT NOTE**: Doing the reading after class is *not* the same as waiting until right before the exam to do it. You've got to spread it out and study a little at a time, not cram it all in the day before the test. (More on this later.)

Now don't get me wrong—if you can do all the readings before class, that's great, you get a gold star. But this is often the ideal rather than the reality. In college, it's not uncommon to have hundreds of pages of reading each week. You'll go crazy if you try to read every single word, and you probably won't absorb very much.

How to Talk about Your Readings in Class

Do you get tongue-tied in the classroom? Have you done the readings but still don't know what to say? In some classes—particularly seminars in college—participation will count for a lot of your grade, so it's important to make your voice heard. Remember that it's okay if you don't have something brilliant to say; if you've got an idea, don't keep it to yourself. Your teacher will appreciate the effort, and you may find that your input was more insightful than you thought.

Show that you've done the reading by making your comments detailed and specific; if you're discussing a text, strengthen your argument by quoting a line or passage. This is when having taken notes in the margins really pays off. Use them as a guide to quickly find the point you want to talk about.

We all get one sooner or later: the teacher who will call on you even when you're not raising your hand. You grip the edge of your desk in suspense, never knowing when your name will be called. You know that whatever you do, you *must not* make eye contact—this just encourages them. But there must be a better way! What you *should* do is take control of the situation: *volunteer early for a question you know* rather than wait to get called on for one you don't. This tactic will usually protect you from surprise attacks.

Here's an easy way to make smart contributions: when you review your notes before class, pick the best ones and write them down in your notebook. Keep them in reserve for when your teacher asks the class for

Survey Says

Top students tend to be big participators. On a scale of 1 to 5, 43 percent gave themselves a 5 for class participation in high school. In college, 41 percent gave themselves a 4.

comments. If you think of something to say while someone else is talking, make a quick note so you don't forget it and can concentrate on the discussion.

Asking questions is another simple way to get participation credit. It can be about something you're not sure of or a question that invites discussion. Make sure it's insightful, though, not just "So…what'd you all think of the book?"

Last but not least, don't forget to have fun! Courses in which you get to discuss and challenge readings are the highlights of many people's classroom careers. When else will you get to dump on Freud for his theories about the subconscious or debate Platonic realism or defend Catherine for marrying Edgar in *Wuthering Heights*? This is your chance to be an intellectual.

Exercise

Take notes on the following excerpt from Alexis de Tocqueville's *Democracy in America*, as translated by Henry Reeve, using the techniques described in this chapter.[70] Mark up the text as you read and write your comments—questions, ideas, and summary—in the margins.

Another remark, to which we shall hereafter have occasion to recur, is applicable not only to the English, but to the French, the Spaniards, and all the Europeans who successively established themselves in the New World. All these European colonies contained the elements, if not the development, of a complete democracy. Two causes led to this result. It may safely be advanced, that on leaving the mother-country the emigrants had in general no notion of superiority over one another. The happy and the powerful do not go into exile, and there are no surer guarantees of equality among men than poverty and misfortune. It happened, however, on several occasions, that persons of rank were driven to America by political and religious quarrels. Laws were made to establish a gradation of ranks; but it was soon found that the soil of America was opposed to a territorial aristocracy. To bring that refractory land into cultivation, the constant and interested exertions of the owner himself were necessary; and when the ground was prepared, its produce was found to be insufficient to enrich a master and a farmer at the same time. The land was then naturally broken up into small portions, which the proprietor cultivated for himself. Land is the basis of an aristocracy, which clings to the soil that supports it; for it is not by privileges alone, nor by birth, but by landed property handed down from generation to generation, that an aristocracy is constituted. A nation may present immense fortunes and extreme wretchedness, but unless those fortunes are territorial there is no aristocracy, but simply the class of the rich and that of the poor.

List three things you could say about the text in class. These can be ideas that occurred to you or questions you had.

1. _____

_____

_____

2. _____

_____

_____

3. _____

_____

_____

H OMEWORK CAN MEAN A lot of things in high school and college. It can be an essay, a problem set, a programming assignment, or even a blog post. It can be big or small, take one day or several weeks, and be worth next to nothing or your entire grade. Whatever kind of homework it is, here's how to get through it with flying colors.

General Homework Tips
Getting Started

I've said it before and I'll say it again: *always read the instructions!* For a complicated assignment, go through it at least two or three times and make sure you know exactly what's required. If you're not sure about something, don't hesitate to ask for help. I've seen students puzzle over vague instructions for hours, when a simple email or visit to the prof's office hours would have cleared everything up.

For practice, take a look at these instructions I got for a computer science group project where we had to build a prototype for an iPad-like device:

> We will assign all members of another team to test your
> team's prototype. You will need to arrange and perform

your tests, noting that all members of your team and exactly one external user from the other team must be present in the room during each test. You are welcome to modify your prototype after (or, in the case of quick minor modifications, during) testing with one of the assigned team members, based on their use of your prototype. The document your team turns in should record this part of the assignment by providing, for each test, copies of the observation index cards written during that test, and a brief overall summary of that test.

Question: How many people have to test your group's prototype? If you said all the members of another team, you get full credit! The answer is right there in the first sentence. Most people in my class, however—including the people in my own group—thought that only *one person* had to test the prototype. When I asked the TA, even he agreed with this (a classic example of why you shouldn't always trust your teaching assistant!). I was so sure I was right that I went up to the professor after class and asked him to confirm my interpretation—which he did, and he proceeded to make an announcement to the entire class.

Once you've got the instructions down, it's time to get to work.

- If you've got a lot of time to complete the assignment, **do a rough draft several days before it's due**. When you come back to it, you'll probably be shocked at how many errors you missed. Save your work on the computer so you can quickly revise.
- Remember that you don't have to do homework at home! This is especially true in college, when you have lots of breaks throughout the day. **Work on it wherever you happen to be, whenever you have the time.**

- Be careful of **making too much out of simple assignments** or questions that aren't worth much. Use your time wisely.
- **Extra-credit assignments** can be lifesavers, but don't do them if it'll take time away from your regular schoolwork or keep you from getting a good night's sleep. Save the extra stuff for last.
- Why is it that high school and college students have the latest high-tech gadgets, but so few of them seem to own staplers? People were always asking to borrow my portable one before handing in assignments. So a little reminder couldn't hurt: **always staple your homework!** Some teachers deduct points if you don't, plus you run the risk that your pages will get separated.
- There are two philosophies about homework (and work in general): get the big things out of the way, or do the little things first. If you're having trouble getting started, or if you're feeling overwhelmed, go for the latter. If you're energetic and alert, or if you're really low on time, you should do the former.

In Their Own Words
"When dealing with homework, do the easy stuff first, so you do not get bogged down on more difficult material and then [get] too tired to finish the easy stuff."

—Top student at Columbia

The Power of Paper

Many teachers have joined the environmental movement by posting assignments online instead of making copies for the class. This is all well and good for Mother Earth, but it may not be the best thing for your GPA. Think of all the things you can do with a hard copy. You can mark it up. You're more likely to read it if it's lying right in front of you. You can take it anywhere you go—like places that are away from the distractions of the Internet. You don't have to bother navigating to the class website and opening a pdf every time you want to look at it. For all these reasons, it's good to print out your homework instructions—you can recycle later.

Tip for foreign language homework. If you're doing a writing assignment for a low-level class, don't try to write what you would in English. Keep the language at the same level as the chapter you're reading in the textbook; it's okay if it sounds as though a third-grader or even a kindergartner wrote it. ("I have a bird. His name is Mark and he is green…") In most cases, the grader will deduct for mistakes, not give you extra points for difficulty.

STEM Homework Strategies

The points above still apply, but the following tips are specific to STEM:

- **Don't dive into your homework without preparation.** Start by reviewing the relevant textbook chapter and your notes, and make sure you can solve the sample problems before tackling the assignment.
- If your teacher or TA, or both, have office hours, **start the assignment before this time so you can go to them for help** if you're stuck.
- In a lot of STEM classes, the teacher will announce that your lowest homework grade(s) will be dropped. **Don't let this lure you into skipping an assignment.** Homework is one of the best ways to pick up STEM concepts, so you're not doing yourself any favors by omitting one. You may think that you'll cover the material on your own time, but it rarely works out that way. Plus, you never know when an assignment at the end of the

term will really throw you for a loop, making you wish you had done that über-easy one a few weeks back.

The odds are in your favor. In many math and science textbooks, the odd-numbered questions are more like part of the lesson than a test of your knowledge. That's because the answers to these questions, along with detailed explanations, are often found in the back of the book or on the publisher's website. These solutions can do wonders for clarifying vague statements in the textbook. Perhaps more importantly, they provide fantastic clues for the even-numbered questions your teacher assigns for homework—so if you're stuck on number 18, check out 17 first!

Grappling with Group Projects

Ah, group projects. Some people love 'em, some people hate 'em—okay, most people hate 'em. Your grade now depends on *other people* whom you may never have met before, and you've somehow got to do the impossible: find some time when a bunch of super-busy high school or college students can actually meet in person. But group projects can also be fun and rewarding, and they're excellent examples of how the "real world" works.

To break the ice, have your first meeting in a casual spot like a café, a park, or a pizza place. Exchange contact information right away, and decide on a topic if you haven't been assigned one. Make sure you have the instructions for the project in front of you at each meeting. (Print them out.) Break up the work so everyone has a part to do—allowing members to choose what to work on as much as possible, based on their strengths and interests—and have regular meetings to check on progress. Since group work can get messy, set a deadline for several days prior to the actual due date. This gives you some leeway if things go awry.

> Don't forget to **thank the people in your group** for their hard work! A simple thank you goes a long way.

Is someone in your group AWOL? Try working it out with them first—ask what's going on, remind them to come to meetings, tell them the group is depending on them—then inform your teacher if there's no improvement. With a little luck they'll come around. However, don't wait too long to redistribute the work among the remaining members.

People who don't pull their weight aren't the only ones you have to worry about. Keep an eye out for the following troublemakers: those who don't read the instructions carefully, those who have impressive but overly ambitious ideas, and those who jump around from topic to topic without ever finishing an idea. If you notice any of these people in your group, be polite without being a pushover. Say something like, "I think building a full-scale model of the Eiffel Tower out of paper clips is a great idea, Cathy, but I'm a little concerned about whether we can do it in the time we have."

> **Technology** can be a big help for group work, and many free applications are available. You can share, edit, and track changes on reports with Google Docs, and create a group schedule using Google Calendar. Start a private group on Facebook so you can post messages and updates to one another. For storing and sharing large files, use Dropbox (www.dropbox.com). MeetingWizard (www.meetingwizard.com) can help find a meeting time that makes everyone happy—but if people have trouble attending in person, they can lend their virtual presence through Skype.

CHAPTER 8

How to Write a Paper

WRITING A PAPER IS a lot like doing a pentathlon—you've got to be very good at a wide range of things. It requires time management, research skills, creativity, logic, persuasive writing, and much, much more. This is your time to shine as a scholar and to think of things no one has ever thought of before. Perhaps more than any test, a paper demonstrates your knowledge of a subject and your ability to apply that knowledge. While the process of putting words to paper is never easy, in the end you've got a document that is uniquely yours and which, hopefully, you can be proud of for years to come.

This chapter is going to focus on papers that require a *thesis*— that is, a statement you have to prove. Many papers in high school and almost every paper in college will call for some kind of thesis. They can be research papers, persuasive essays, opinion pieces, literary analyses, and more. I'm not going to talk about things like summaries, newspaper-style articles, descriptive pieces, or creative writing, which require a very different skill set.

Step 1: Getting On Board with Guidelines

If your teacher gave you the assignment orally, write down each and every requirement; if he or she gave you written guidelines, read them at least two or three times. Remember that your grade will be based not just on the quality of the paper, but on how well you follow instructions. Don't disqualify yourself from an A before you've even started! Make sure you're crystal clear on the following:

- How many words or pages are required? Is there a range?
- Is there a specific question (a prompt) that needs to be answered?
- Does it have to be on a certain topic?
- What types of sources are required, if any? Should the paper be based on specific texts or are you free to choose your own? Will you need primary and secondary sources?
- How many sources are required, if any? Do you have to do outside research, or is it based on readings that were assigned for class?
- Does your teacher want footnotes, endnotes, or in-text citations? What format should they be in?
- Do you have to submit a thesis or draft of your paper before the final version?
- Did your teacher provide a recommended bibliography?
- And last but certainly not least—when is it due?

Step 2: Choosing a Topic

Sometimes your teacher will make life easier by telling you what to write about. Sure, you may not always *like* the topic, but at least this saves you the trouble of having to think of one by yourself. Plus, whether the topic is easy or hard, all your classmates will be in the same boat. If your teacher gives you a list of topics to choose from, go for one that's highly specific with well-defined parameters. If possible, stay away from the most obvious choice—the one everybody else seems to be doing. Your teacher will probably appreciate a change of pace when he or she is pulling a marathon all-night grading session.

If the burden is all on you, though, you've got a big decision to make. The topic you choose can mean the difference between an incredibly frustrating, tear-your-hair-out experience and a paper that practically writes itself. Here's how to pick a good one.

- **Did something jump out at you earlier in the term?** Something that made you stop and think, "I would really like to know more about this," or "That explanation the teacher gave didn't sound quite right." Make a list of these things as you encounter them; don't wait until the paper assignment is announced. You should be on the lookout for potential paper topics from day one of the semester.
- Don't know where to start? **Read through your class notes and syllabus to give your brain a refresher.** If your teacher posed a question but never answered it, or mentioned a topic but never fleshed it out, this may be a paper just waiting to happen.
- **Review your textbook and other reading assignments.** Be on the lookout for topics that cry out for more attention and for statements that are ambiguous, simplistic, contradictory, or controversial. Some textbooks have questions for further discussion at the end of each section—they're practically giving paper topics away!
- **Go over past assignments.** Are there any questions that could do with further investigation, or that could be applied to another area? When you got the assignment back, did your teacher make a thought-provoking comment on what you wrote?
- **Use Wikipedia for a whirlwind introduction to potential topics.** Click on the hyperlinks whenever you come across a term you'd like to know more about, and see where your curiosity leads you. There are often excellent external links at the

bottom of each page. *Warning:* Unless your teacher says it's okay, do *not* cite Wikipedia in your paper.

- **Ask your teacher for suggestions.** This is best done after you've put some thought into the matter, though, as most teachers don't like giving out paper topics for free. Remember to bring along a notebook to write down his or her advice.

Be Specific

In general, the narrower your focus, the better your paper will be. So if you're feeling overwhelmed by a topic, try cutting it down to a more manageable size. Here are some examples of how to turn a nebulous idea into a highly refined, easily researchable paper topic.

Sample Paper Topics	
General	**Specific**
The Cuban missile crisis	Robert McNamara's role in the Cuban missile crisis
Buddhism	The practice of Buddhism in modern-day India
Advertising	Advertising aimed at preteen girls in America

Suit the Paper to the Time

Say you have this really exciting, first-rate idea, one you know your teacher would love and which no one has ever thought of before. The only problem is that you would need weeks to research and write it—and the paper's due in ten days! Judging what you can do in the time you have is an important skill in school and in life, and it's part of what you're being graded on.

Unfortunately, your teacher won't give you an A just for having a brilliant idea. If you can't do your topic justice, you'd better find something else to write about. I'm not saying you should give up on it, just that you can find better venues. If you're in high school, consider taking a class in college where you can give your idea the attention it deserves. If you're in college now, you could incorporate it into your senior thesis or even save it for grad school. For now, see if you can write your paper on a smaller part of your overarching idea.

How I chose my senior thesis topic. When I started my last year of college, I had no idea what to write about for my senior thesis. (In case you were wondering, a senior thesis is typically a very long paper that requires a lot of independent research and that may be required for your major.) My only guideline was that I was specializing in medieval European history. I quickly narrowed it down to medieval English history because most of the secondary sources are in English, and my foreign language skills weren't good enough to cope with the French, Italian, or German I would need to do research on other countries. I eventually settled on the English Peasants' Revolt of 1381 (ever heard of it?) for a number of reasons: there was a fair amount written on the subject but not too much; there were only a handful of primary sources, written in Latin or Middle English, and these were all available in translation at my library; I was interested in the lives of the peasantry of the Middle Ages; and the subject of a revolt sounded exciting. Once I chose my topic, everything seemed to fall into place.

Step 3: Going on a Research Crusade

As you've probably guessed, this step applies only to research papers. It's become incredibly easy to find information online, but a lot of sources are still only available in hard copy. To find the books you need, do a search on your school or local library's online catalog, or better yet, physically go to the library and ransack the shelves. Look at all the titles and skim through the ones that pique your interest; you'll find stuff you never would have known existed with an online search alone.

Google can be a great research aid, but be very careful about citing websites in your paper. If an article on the Web refers to a source, you should find and cite the original text rather than footnoting the website. Sites affiliated with universities are usually trustworthy. If you're not sure whether websites are off-limits for your paper, ask your teacher. With that caveat, here are **six tips for smart googling**:

1. Use double quotes to search for an exact term or a set of words in a specific order.
2. If you want to exclude results that contain a certain term, put a hyphen before that term in your search. For example, *Children's Crusade -Vonnegut* will search for the medieval crusade, not the Kurt Vonnegut novel of the same name.
3. Include "site:" to limit your search to a particular website (*site:nytimes.com*) or top-level domain (*site:.edu*).
4. If you're looking for pdf documents—which are often more scholarly than regular websites—enter your search term followed by "filetype:pdf."
5. Check out Google Scholar at http://scholar.google.com/. Doing a search here will bring up lots of academic articles and online books. Even if you don't have full access to them, you can often view enough to get some really great quotes and ideas. *Quick tip*: To do a search by author, type "author:name." For example, author:stone will show you works by Stone rather than articles about rocks.
6. When trying to find a term on a web page, don't forget about good old Ctrl-F (or Command-F if you use a Mac). Just type

the word or phrase you want to find in the box that pops up, and it'll show you all the places where it occurs.

Academic databases are another fantastic—and much more trustworthy—electronic research tool. They aren't free, but a lot of colleges provide their students with access. The database JSTOR is one of the best research tools ever—by plugging in a few terms, you can see over a century's worth of articles from academic journals. (You should focus on the newer ones, though, since a lot can change in a hundred years—even in topics like ancient history.) Reading through articles is a whole lot faster than slogging through entire books. You can also get a whirlwind introduction to a lot of texts by reading people's reviews. Some other good databases are ProQuest, EBSCO, SpringerLink, LexisNexis (good for legal and public-records information), and ScienceDirect. For articles you can access for free, check out DOAJ (Directory of Open Access Journals).

A lot of students skip over footnotes (or endnotes) when they read, but they're actually passing up a fantastic resource. These notes are like graveyards for the authors' half-finished ideas and unproven theories, things that weren't needed for their own papers. *This makes footnotes an excellent source of inspiration.*

Take, for example, an article about the ancient synagogue of Dura Europos in modern-day Syria. The authors state in their very first footnote, "The art of the synagogue will not be dealt with in this paper, except in as much as it relates directly to the discussion. Nor will the evidence from the brief, final period of the synagogue's existence in the second half of the third century: both subjects warrant separate discussions."[71] And there you have it, two potential papers just waiting to be written.

At this point you should be skimming books and articles—don't spend hours reading one text before you've even come up with a thesis. Focus on the chapters and passages you find most interesting.

You'll probably start to notice that a lot of authors cite the same sources again and again and again. For every topic, a handful of texts make up essential reading—make sure you take a look at these sources for yourself.

Step 4: Coming Up with a Thesis

Okay, so you've decided on a topic, raided the library, maybe paid a little visit to your teacher. It's now time for the most crucial and dreaded part of the paper-writing process: finding a thesis. A thesis, by the way, is the argument you'll be proving in your paper, and it is the bane of many students' existences. Your mission is to come up with an original, meaningful statement about your topic and then use evidence to back it up. This evidence can come in the form of facts, statistics, passages or quotations from a text, studies, experiments, class notes, art and artifacts, interviews, personal experience, and more.

The Top Ten Qualities of a Good Thesis

1. It must be specific.
2. It must take a stand on something.
3. It should not state the obvious.
4. It must be something you can prove (and that requires proving).
5. It should be objective—unless you're writing an opinion piece.
6. It should answer a question, but not a "yes or no" question.
7. It should be one sentence long—although for longer, more complex papers, it's okay if it's several lines or even a full paragraph.
8. If you're responding to a prompt (a question posed by the teacher), your thesis must directly answer the prompt.
9. It should not state absolutes or superlatives—for example, "Napoleon was the best general ever because...."
10. It's often helpful to include a counterargument as part of

your thesis. A counterargument is a statement that your thesis will reject or refine. For example: "While scholars such as Henry and James assert that the island of Keos was under Mycenaean hegemony in the Late Bronze Age, new archaeological evidence reveals that it was actually a Minoan colony at this time." By stating the counterargument, you help to strengthen and give purpose to your own argument.

Remember those topics I mentioned earlier? Here are some potential thesis statements that could come out of them.

| Sample Thesis Statements ||
Topic	Thesis
Robert McNamara's role in the Cuban missile crisis	Although some scholars claim that JFK prevented nuclear war from breaking out during the Cuban missile crisis, Robert McNamara actually played a more crucial role in the successful resolution of the conflict.
The practice of Buddhism in modern-day India	The rise of Buddhism among the native population of northern India in the late twentieth century was spurred by the exile of the Dalai Lama to Dharamsala.
Advertising aimed at preteen girls in America	Although most parents believe that advertising hurts preteen girls' self-image, commercials aimed at young girls actually improve their self-esteem by giving them positive role models.

If you're lucky, your thesis will come to you in a flash of inspiration. Other times, no matter how hard you rack your brains, the lightbulb just never seems to go off. But never fear—there are plenty of things you can do to force inspiration.

Create a Research Log

One of the best ways to come up with a thesis is to create a log of your research. Whether you're looking at one book or twenty, you should write down any quotations, facts, and ideas that strike you—even though you haven't decided on a thesis yet. For each thing you write down, be sure to include the title of the book or article and the page number it comes from. Make note of any and all of the following:

- Useful background information.
- Your responses/reactions to what you're reading.
- Anything you agree or disagree with.
- Anything that needs clarification.
- Statements that are overly conventional.
- Statements that are controversial.
- Holes in the authors' arguments.
- Statements in which authors contradict each other or themselves.

These last four are excellent starting points for a thesis. They're practically begging for readers to challenge them.

You don't have to go into a lot of detail in your research log. For example, if you come across statistics on the number of Americans who had electricity at the turn of the twentieth century, and you think this might be good to cite in a paper, just write, "Page 23—# Americans w/electricity." You can always go back to the text and look up the actual figures. If the precise wording is important, though, you should probably include the whole quotation.

As you read your sources, remember that you are now a scholar. Think of academia as a perpetual back-and-forth debate. Just because you're in high school or college doesn't mean you can't come up with a better solution than people with advanced degrees. It's perfectly valid to come up with a thesis that sets out to disprove a previously accepted theory.

Although you're a scholar, you should also act like a two-year-old—always ask "Why?" Get into the habit of constantly questioning your sources. Read with a critical eye, and never take what anyone says for granted. Ask yourself questions like: What were the author's motives or biases? How does the author know this? Does this argument make sense? Why did this historical figure or character do what he or she did? Why did this event happen at this time?

I found my inspiration for my paper on the Peasants' Revolt of 1381 when I read this rather startling admission by one historian:

> Without any articulated decision, without even any very extended argument, study of the revolt has come almost to ignore chronicle narratives in favor of judicial evidence. This historiographic turn has produced brilliant results for understanding the economic conditions..., the social composition of the rebel bands, and the chronology of the rising itself; but something has also been lost, a curiosity about what drove the rebels, about what they thought and what they wanted.[72]

Once I read this, I pretty much knew what to do for my thesis: since most scholars had been ignoring the chronicle narratives, I would make them my focus; and since most historians had lost their curiosity about what drove the rebels, I would try to get into the minds of these fourteenth-century English peasants.

Why Are Research Logs Important?

Two main reasons:

1. **Creating a research log makes it easier to see the big picture.** When you're in the middle of a book, you may be too focused on what you're reading to put the information in context. But when you review these notes once or twice or three times, a theme or pattern will start to emerge. Having all these important points in one place can help you make connections and observations.

2. **When you're writing the paper, you'll be able to cite your sources without going on a wild-goose chase for half-remembered quotes and figures.** You'll also know exactly where to go if you need to clarify something.

It's a good idea to do your research log on the computer, for a number of reasons. You'll be able to easily search for terms—a huge plus when it comes to making connections and finding citations for a paper—and you can write out quotations faster. If you do additional research, you can add to your log and move things around. And when you're writing the paper, you can simply copy and paste quotes and other information.

Step 5: Getting Ready to Write

Congratulations, you've found your thesis! The hardest part is over. But don't start celebrating just yet. If you're doing a research paper, it may be time to make another trip to the stacks. Now that you know what you're trying to prove, ask yourself whether you really have enough evidence to make your case. Be on the lookout for holes in your argument and for counterarguments you must address.

Your searches will probably be more directed and focused now, since you have a better idea of what you're looking for. Sometimes, with databases like JSTOR, you can find what you need in seconds. Use the advanced search functionality in your library's online catalog. It usually will allow you to search for multiple terms and mix and match your search by keyword, title, author, subject, and so on. As you do this second round of research, make sure to update your research log.

Before you start writing, it's time to make a plan—otherwise known as an outline. For a short paper (under three pages), write

You've been racking your brains for hours, have read your research log about ten times, and still no thesis. If you keep this up much longer, your head is going to explode. What's a poor student to do? The answer is: **anything but keep thinking about your thesis**. Many people find that their best ideas come to them while they're doing something completely unrelated. Go for a walk, exercise, take a shower, do work for another class, chat with a friend—whatever it takes to get your mind off your topic. There's also something to the old adage of "just sleep on it." Your brain often makes connections while you're asleep that eluded you in your conscious state. **Hint:** Always carry around a pen and a pad of paper. You never know when inspiration will strike!

down how each paragraph is going to support your thesis. For a longer paper, just sketch out the flow of your argument. Note each point you're going to make and where it will occur; and for each point, list the evidence that supports it. This is when having prepared a research log really pays off: use it to find quotes, facts, and figures to back up your thesis.

> When you write a paper, think of yourself as a lawyer making your case before the judge. Only instead of getting your client off, your reward will be getting an A: "Your honor, I intend to show that my client, Julius Caesar, was not responsible for the dissolution of the Roman Republic..."

What's in a Point?

A point is a sub-argument that supports your thesis (the main argument) by providing evidence, refuting counterarguments, and making logical deductions. Let's return to our examples for a moment and add some points for each one. (These are completely made up, by the way—I haven't actually researched them—so think twice before you use them for a real paper.)

Sample Thesis Points	
Thesis	**Points**
Although some scholars claim that JFK prevented nuclear war from breaking out during the Cuban missile crisis, Robert McNamara actually played a more crucial role in the successful resolution of the conflict.	• Transcripts show that JFK deferred to McNamara during key stages of the conflict. • McNamara had more direct contact with Castro and Khrushchev than JFK did. • JFK's original plan was very different from the one he adopted after consulting with McNamara, and could have worsened the conflict.
The rise of Buddhism among the native population of northern India in the late twentieth century was spurred by the exile of the Dalai Lama to Dharamsala.	• The number of northern Indians who practice Buddhism began to rise immediately after the exile. • Northern Indians have frequent interactions with exiled Tibetans. • The type of Buddhism practiced by northern Indians bears more resemblance to Tibetan Buddhism than that practiced elsewhere in India.

(continues)

| Sample Thesis Points, cont. ||
Thesis	Points
Although most parents believe that advertising hurts preteen girls' self-image, commercials aimed at young girls actually improve their self-esteem by giving them positive role models.	• According to a study, preteen girls exhibit higher levels of self-esteem after watching age-appropriate commercials. • Most of the commercials aimed at preteen girls portray strong female characters. • The majority of parents cannot describe a single commercial currently aimed at preteen girls.

Step 6: Writing the Paper (Finally)

Most papers follow a certain pattern—most teachers will expect it, and it makes the writing easier, too. In the first paragraph, build up to your thesis by providing background information, setting up a counterargument that you'll be rejecting, defining key terms, putting your thesis in context, analyzing a quote from one of your sources, or posing a question that your thesis will answer.

Your thesis should usually come at the end of the first paragraph, but if your paper is very long—say, a fifty-plus-page monster of a senior thesis—you might want to wait until the end of the first section or chapter. Occasionally people will write open-form essays, in which the thesis isn't stated until the end of the paper. Most teachers will expect to see it in the beginning, though, so it's best not to keep them waiting.

In the body of your paper, be sure to *use connecting sentences.* Every paragraph (except the first) should begin with a topic sentence that links the current paragraph to the one before it. Draw your reader from one paragraph to the next in a clear, logical fashion with words such as "however," "moreover," "while," "nevertheless," "in addition," "also," "indeed," "for example," "since," "then," "because," and "although." Don't make your reader guess where you're going!

Every paragraph should play a unique role in supporting your thesis and should clearly relate to your central argument. Make sure that all of your points are relevant and on topic, and keep in mind that a really strong essay will not only provide evidence in support of your thesis, but also address and refute counterarguments.

Follow your outline as much as you can, but realize that it's okay if your paper doesn't adhere to it completely. Think of your paper as a living, breathing thing. One paragraph will often give rise to the next in an organic, natural growth that can be hard to predict. You may think of things that never would've occurred to you before you started writing.

The final paragraph is a bit tricky. Gone are the days when you can simply summarize what you said in your paper. In general, *your conclusion should recap your argument and go a little bit further*—it should leave the reader with something to think about. Here are some suggestions for ending your paper with a bang:

- Address the consequences or implications of your argument. For example: given my findings about McNamara's role in the Cuban missile crisis, his performance as Secretary of Defense must be reevaluated.
- Propose steps for additional research.
- Put it into a broader context. For example: the fact that commercials aimed at preteen girls improve their self-esteem is part of a broader movement among advertisers to empower women.
- Mention new questions that your conclusion has raised.

- Explain the significance of your findings. For example: my finding that the rise of Buddhism in northern India was spurred by the exile of the Dalai Lama is important because it gives us a better understanding of the diversity of religion in India.

- Discuss the limitations of your thesis. Be careful with this one, though, as you don't want to make it sound like you're contradicting yourself.

To see these techniques in action, check out the sample essay at the end of this chapter.

Unfortunately, many people suffer from *BPS—Blank Page Syndrome*. Let's face it: starting to write is scary. Seeing the cursor blinking at you on that bright white screen, realizing that you now have to come up with three or ten or twenty pages of text all on your own—it's enough to give anyone a major case of writer's block. But don't despair! There are plenty of things you can do to ease into writing, such as telling yourself it's okay to make mistakes. Writing is like painting: you can always go back and change something you're not happy with. It doesn't have to be perfect the first time—just make sure you leave enough time for revision! You can even pull a James Joyce and start off with a quick stream-of-consciousness draft. Write down whatever comes into your head without thinking about how it sounds—you can do some major adding and editing later. Most importantly, *start your paper early* so you don't feel compelled to write the whole thing in one sitting. It's much less intimidating if you only have to do a page at a time.

You can also conquer BPS by *starting with the easy stuff*. If you're doing a research paper, consider doing the bibliography or Works Cited page first. Write down all your sources in a format such as APA or MLA—your teacher may tell you which one to use. This takes some of the pressure off because you're no longer staring at an empty page, and you're getting a small but necessary part of your paper out of the way. I always like doing the little things first so I can head into the real job with a feeling of accomplishment.

> Here's a good rule of thumb: don't use a direct quote more than once every two or three paragraphs, and don't use a block quote more than once every few pages. You should use a quotation only if the precise wording matters, if it explains something far better than you could do it yourself, or if it's a piece of evidence from a primary source. If you paraphrase a quote, don't forget to footnote it.

Another way to start is by *writing out quotations, facts and figures, and any other supporting information you want to use from your research log,* in the order you plan to cite them. Once you have your evidence laid out, you can write your paper around them. Keep in mind, though, that your paper shouldn't sound like one long list of citations; you must logically connect these pieces of evidence and explain how they're relevant to your argument.

A few words of advice about the writing process itself. *If you can't think of exactly the right word, don't try to force it*—just leave it blank and come back to it later. I like to insert brackets with possible words or ellipses, which I put in bold so I can easily find them. Racking your brain for the perfect word wastes too much time and energy. Besides, it'll probably pop into your head when you least expect it.

Similarly, don't waste time debating whether or not to delete things. Sometimes it can be hard to take out words, sentences, or even complete paragraphs that you've worked so hard on. You know they don't quite work, but you're not ready to delete them forever. Who knows, maybe you'll change your mind or be able to use them somewhere else. Take the temporary measure of cutting and pasting them into the bottom of your paper, or putting them in italics.

You should, however, waste no time in getting rid of unneeded words. A lot of students have a field day with adjectives and adverbs—they confuse flowery prose with good writing. But your work will be stronger without these distractions.

Step 7: Revise, Revise, Revise

Make sure you leave plenty of time to edit your paper. No matter how good your thesis is, your teacher probably won't take it seriously if it doesn't sound polished. It would be a pity to spend so much time crafting a paper, only to miss out on the grade you deserve due to clunky writing. When you revise, it's helpful to print it out. Many people (myself included) find it easier to read and make comments on a hard copy, and it's amazing how different your writing will sound on paper than on a computer screen. Write your edits on the printout, then go to the computer and implement all changes at the same time.

You should also *get a fresh pair of eyes*. It's hard to view your own writing objectively. After all, this is your baby—you created it, nourished it, made sure it didn't hit its head on the table, etc. That's why you should ask a friend or family member to read it and give you feedback. Sometimes teachers or teaching assistants are willing to give your draft a quick read-through. If that's the case, make sure you take advantage of this special, limited-time offer. Who better to give you advice on a paper than the person who's going to be grading it?

The Next Day Rule. Get a good night's sleep before you start revising. You'll see your paper differently in the morning.

How to Budget Your Time

It takes a lot of steps to write a paper, so the first thing you should do when you get the assignment is make a schedule. The following is what I recommend for a typical research paper. You can adjust these percentages depending on the nature of the project and your strengths and weaknesses—for example, if you're a fast writer, you might want to spend more time on research and less on writing.

- Time spent deciding on a topic (if it's not already given): 5 percent
- Time spent doing research, creating a research log, and coming up with a thesis: 30 percent
- Time spent creating outline and doing any remaining/follow-up research: 10 percent
- Time spent writing the paper: 45 percent
- Time spent revising the paper and getting feedback: 10 percent

Let's say you're given a start date of October 1 and a deadline of October 31:

Sample Paper Schedule			
Task	Percentage of Total Time	Number of Days Based on 30 Total	Completion Date Given Start of October 1
Deciding on a topic (if it's not already given)	5 percent	1.5	October 3
Doing research, creating a research log, and coming up with a thesis	30 percent	9	October 12

(continues)

Sample Paper Schedule, cont.			
Task	Percentage of Total Time	Number of Days Based on 30 Total	Completion Date Given Start of October 1
Creating outline and doing any remaining or follow-up research	10 percent	3	October 15
Writing the paper	45 percent	13.5	October 28
Revising the paper and getting feedback	10 percent	3	October 31
Happy Halloween! Now get a costume and go party!			

Six Grammatical Mistakes You Should Never, Ever, Not in a Million, Billion Years, Make in Your Papers

The following might sound obvious to some of you, but I've seen people with advanced degrees make these mistakes—heck, I've even seen professors make them—so it couldn't hurt to go over a few basic grammar rules.

1. **Your vs. You're**

    Your: Second person possessive adjective, describes something as belonging to you, almost always followed by a noun.

    You're: The contraction of "you are."

Teacher: I loved reading *your* paper on the transport of giant stone money to the island of Yap.

You: Awww, *you're* too kind!

2. Its vs. It's

It's: The contraction of "it is" or "it has."

Its: Possessive adjective meaning "of it" or "belonging to it."

Teacher: *Its* grammar is flawless.

You: Well, you know, *it's* not hard, once you know the rules.

3. There vs. Their vs. They're

Their: Third-person plural possessive adjective meaning "of them" or "belonging to them," almost always followed by a noun.

They're: The contraction of "they are."

There can indicate a place, introduce a noun or clause, be used for emphasis, or mean the opposite of "here."

Teacher: *They're* doing a reading of student papers down at the local Y.

You: Oh, you mean that Y *there*? [pointing]

Teacher: Yes. *Their* events are very well attended.

4. Who's vs. Whose

Who's: The contraction of "who is" or "who has."

Whose: The possessive form of "who."

You: *Who's* going to do the readings?

Teacher: Every student *whose* paper scored an A or higher.

5. **Who vs. Whom**

Who: A subject, the person performing the action of the verb.

Whom: An object, the person to, about, or for whom the action is being done. *Whom* often occurs after a preposition such as "to," "with," and "from."

The who/whom rule. Here's an easy way to know which one to use. If you can substitute "he," "she," or "they" for the word, use *who*. If it makes more sense with "him," "her," or "them," use *whom*.

Teacher: *Who* inspired you to write about this subject? [Using the who/whom rule: "*He* inspired me…"]

You: My father is the person to *whom* I am most indebted. [Using the who/whom rule: "I am most indebted to *him*."]

6. **Then vs. Than**

Than: A conjunction used in comparisons.

Then can mean "at that point in time," "next," "in addition," "also," "in that case, "therefore."

The bottom line is that if you're not comparing something, use *then*.

Teacher: *Then* you'll be inviting him to the reading?

You: Yes, I would rather invite him *than* anyone in the world.

Sample Paper

The following is an excerpt from a paper I wrote in response to the following prompt:

Historians, philosophers, art historians, and legions of students have pondered what can be called "the Renaissance problem." Did a distinct period of innovation, or rebirth, actually occur in Europe in the fifteenth and early sixteenth century? Your task is to enter the debate and think up your own position on the issue. Would you subscribe to the belief that there *was* such a period as the Renaissance? How would you define it? Or conversely, how would you defend the argument to "de-periodize" this era of history?

I chose to do the latter, partly because I felt that few of my classmates would be attempting this. It's worth noting that **this paper did *not* require any outside research**; I had to limit myself to sources that were assigned as part of the course. This was a key parameter, turning what could have been an extremely open-ended subject into a manageable essay.

The Myth of the Renaissance

The term Renaissance, or "rebirth," implies a sudden and drastic change in the status quo. It suggests that what did not exist in one moment appeared in full force in the next, that the time before the fifteenth and early sixteenth centuries—known as the Middle Ages—was devoid of progress, and that it was a phenomenon affecting virtually all parts of society. However, history is rarely so black and white. As we shall see, it is inaccurate to say that there was such a period as the

By defining the term Renaissance, I set up the counterargument I will be arguing against.

Renaissance; instead, it should be viewed as the continuation of a gradual process of innovation and change.

Humanism, an intellectual movement that is almost synonymous with the Renaissance, appeared in Europe long before the fifteenth century. Rhetoricians were already promoting an important humanist ideal, "that education should be reformed to give more attention to the classics and to help people lead moral lives," in the late thirteenth century (Chambers et al. 394).[73] Byzantine scholars, who played a major role in reintroducing the Greek language to Western Europe, had been coming to Italy since the late fourteenth century (Chambers et al. 385). And one of the most prominent humanists, Petrarch, worked and died in the 1300s. To be sure, this movement spread more quickly and gathered greater force in the fifteenth and sixteenth centuries, but it had its roots in the Middle Ages.

It can also be said that there was no such period as the Renaissance because the innovations of the fifteenth and sixteenth centuries affected only a small portion of the population. The condition of the peasantry, for example, may actually have worsened at this time. While

See how each sentence in this paragraph builds up to my thesis, which is stated here. I'm arguing against a commonly accepted belief, and I'm responding directly to the prompt. There's nothing off topic here.

The first sentence makes it clear how this paragraph supports my argument.

Here I approach my argument from a different angle: the Renaissance had a limited reach.

society had been relatively stable from the Early Middle Ages until the fourteenth century, numerous peasant revolts against the propertied class occurred in the following two centuries (Chambers et al. 368). Thomas More's *Utopia* also makes reference to the plight of the poor in Renaissance Europe. According to the character Raphael, "nobles and gentlemen" enclosed "all the land they [could] for pasture," thus evicting "hundreds of farmers" who "[couldn't] find anywhere else to live" (46–47; bk. 1). These displaced farmers lived on the margins of society, forced to steal or beg in order to survive. The intellectual movements of the elites had little or no impact on the lives of these peasants.

I use a contemporary source, which we discussed in class, to spice things up a bit; until now I've only been citing secondary sources.

Although the developments of the fifteenth and sixteenth centuries were outgrowths of the Middle Ages, and despite the fact that they had limited impact on Europeans as a whole, this age was certainly not without its merits; it improved upon earlier inventions and produced its own novel ideas. Humanism may have had its roots in the Middle Ages, for example, but it was not fully developed until the fifteenth and sixteenth centuries. While monks and Scholastics monopolized medieval learning, Renaissance humanism introduced a large portion of lay society to the "intellectual treasury of the European past" (Chambers 399); and civic humanism, which promoted participation in public affairs, originated in Italy in the 1400s. The printing press, which had an undeniable impact on the progress of Western culture, was perfected in the mid-fifteenth century. Yet another innovation was the belief that females should be educated. In light of this evidence, it can be said that the fifteenth and sixteenth centuries witnessed not a "rebirth" of culture, but a maturation of the one that already existed.

> In this concluding paragraph, I do more than summarize my argument—I refine it by showing its limitations. I admit that there were significant innovations and improvements in the period known as the Renaissance, but in the end I return to my thesis.

Exercise

For each of the topics listed below, write down a more specific topic that could come out of it, a potential thesis statement, and three points you could make in support of your thesis. (Note: you can make up anything you want—this is just for practice.)

Tip: Your thesis should be something worth proving; avoid stating the obvious.

Topic 1: Feudalism

More Specific Topic: _____

Thesis: _____

_____

_____

_____

Point 1: _____

Point 2: _____

Point 3: _____

Topic 2: Global Warming

More Specific Topic: _____

Thesis:

_____

_____

_____

_____

Point 1: _____

Point 2: _____

Point 3: _____

Topic 3: Japan

More Specific Topic: _____

Thesis:

_____

_____

_____

_____

Point 1: _____

Point 2: _____

Point 3: _____

CHAPTER 9

Getting Ready for the Test

"I have no idea what's going to be on the exam."

"I just don't test well."

"Those questions really caught me by surprise."

"I can't seem to think fast enough on exams."

"I don't know how to prepare for this test."

"I can't control how I do on tests—sometimes I get lucky, sometimes I don't."

"I crammed so hard for this exam, but then I blanked out."

"That test was really long—I just made up answers for the last section."

"I thought I got it right, but when I asked Tom, he got something totally different, so now I don't know."

"I read all the assigned material—I don't know why I didn't do better."

"I could've done better if I had more time to study."

Do any of these sound familiar to you? They're common sentiments among students, but they're not things that you should be saying. Believing that you're not a good test-taker, that you can't predict what's going to be on the exam, or that you have no control over the situation are self-fulfilling prophecies. Because guess what: you can become a better test-taker, and you *are* in control over your test destiny.

Am I saying that exams are never unfair or that there are some things you just can't prepare for? No, of course not. But taking a test is like any other skill: it requires preparation, strategy, determination, and lots and lots of practice. Luckily for you, your teachers have taken care of the practice part.

What to Do When the Test Is in Sight

Getting As is about more than understanding the material—you've got to know your test, too. As soon as your teacher announces the exam, make sure you can answer the following questions:

1.   What material will it be on?
2.   Is it cumulative, or is it only on what's been covered since the last test?
3.   How much of your grade is it worth?
4.   What kind of questions will it have—multiple-choice, true/false, short answer, essays, or something else?

Most teachers waste no time providing this information, but if they're keeping mum, don't be afraid to raise your hand or go up to them after class. Just stay away from the all-encompassing question, "What's going to be on the test?" because this sounds like you're looking for the answer key. Questions such as "Will the test be cumulative?" and "What will the format be?" are a bit more polite. Don't panic if your teacher purposefully withholds information. Look at tests from earlier in the semester for clues about format and question types. If it's the first test of the term, be prepared for all contingencies, and remember that your classmates are in the same suspense-filled boat.

When preparing for your test, *don't forget about the syllabus!*

Although your teacher gave it to you a long time ago, it may still have information about what's fair game on exams. You should also reread your notes from the first day of class, as that's when teachers discuss their vision for the rest of the semester.

If you're lucky, your teacher will give you an exam from a previous year. Work out all the problems by yourself under timed conditions, whether or not you already have the answers; and if anything's unclear, ask your teacher, TA, or study group for help. Review these exams at least two or three times, as your test is bound to bear a striking resemblance.

In Their Own Words

"For high grades, learn on the first day what is being evaluated and how previous students taking the same class did well: e.g., study sources they used, practice materials, etc."

—Top student and graduate of Yale University

"If you are given old exams, use this resource. It's usually the best metric for what to expect."

—Goldwater Scholar

Review sessions should really be called "classes where we practically give away what's going to be on the exam." Make sure you attend and take detailed notes.

Looking over tests you took earlier in the semester is one of the best ways to improve your performance on future exams. Read through the comments and examine the questions for patterns and preferences. For example:

- What did your teacher like or dislike about your essays? Should you have included more examples? Did you write too much or not enough? Did you answer the question?
- Are the questions more concerned with the "big picture" than with nuances and details, or vice versa?
- Do you have a tendency to over-analyze questions? Do you look for tricks in the simplest of statements? Most test questions are pretty straightforward, and you may be hurting your grade by reading too much into them.
- Did the true/false questions almost always turn out to be true?
- Were most of the questions based on problems you did in class or for homework?
- Do the exams tend to be on the long or short side? Can you answer the questions at a leisurely pace, or do you have to rush through them with superhuman speed?
- Was everything on the exam covered in class? As discussed earlier, many teachers will test you on something only if it was included in their lecture. This often means you can study exclusively from your notes—if they're detailed enough.

In Their Own Words

"More than the content of the test, it's important to figure out what type of test it is and what you'll be expected to do. For instance, if it's entirely a multiple-choice test, there's likely going to be less analysis required, so pure information- and detail-absorption is usually important. If the test is entirely essay based, you should spend more time thinking about broader concepts and how they relate to another. Unlike in multiple-choice tests, in which you'll be refreshed [on] details as you see them in questions, you should pick important concepts and memorize them for essay-based tests because you're likely not going to be able to remember every detail of every concept. It's all about anticipating what's going to be on the test. To that effect, you should always try to get your hands on the professor's previous tests, if available, or talk to students who have taken the professor's previous exams."

—Yale Law School student

When's the Best Time to Start Studying?

The answer is: before the exam is even announced. How is this possible, you ask? Easy—if you've been keeping up with the homework and readings and reviewing your notes, you've been preparing for this test all along! When you know you have an exam coming up, however, it's time to engage in more directed study. Based on what you know about the class and the test itself, do you have to focus on your notes or your books? Is it a test where you have to know facts as well as concepts? Are all topics equally important, or will some be emphasized more than others? Once you know what you have to study, it's time to…

> ### Survey Says
> Among the high achievers, 82 percent say that they have good intuition about what's going to be on tests. Top students aren't psychic, but they are good observers of what goes on in the classroom. During lectures, they pick up on subtle (and not-so-subtle) clues about what the teacher thinks is important. They know their homework assignments and past tests inside and out. And last but not least, they make sure they know the structure and focus of the exam.

Put Your Brain to Work: The Art of Active Studying

Is your idea of studying rereading your notes and books as many times as humanly possible? When you read, do you stick your head in a book and never come out? If so, you're engaging in something called passive studying, which is a very passé thing to do. Make your study time more productive by actively reviewing the material. Active studying means you *do stuff* to make the information stick, such as asking questions—lots of them—as you review. Questions like:

- What "big idea" does this represent or is this an example of?
- When would I apply this formula?
- What were the causes of this event?
- How does this author compare to others we've read?
- Why is this important?
- What are some examples of this theme?

Some other active learning techniques are *putting key concepts in your own words* and saying them out loud for extra reinforcement, *making diagrams* for complicated processes or visualizing them in your head, and *explaining a concept to somebody else*. For STEM classes, *redo exercises* from class and homework and do additional problems from the book.

In Their Own Words

"Teach your classmates if they need help. Teaching really helps you consolidate what you learn."

–Goldwater Scholar

"Redo all homework assignments. Take as many practice tests as possible."
–Rhodes Scholar and high school valedictorian

"Find what works for you. By that, I don't mean that you should do what's comfortable, but test different techniques and see what improves your scores. Don't just read, unless you have an incredible memory. I learned by doing; practice problems, outlining classes, using flash cards (which are great for language and history classes). Rewrite proofs for math classes."

—Student at Yale Law School

"Find ways of viewing the material from different angles, by reading about it, talking about it, learning from others, teaching others."

—Rhodes Scholar and Goldwater Scholar

Make Review Sheets

One of the best active studying techniques is to create review sheets, which are essentially summaries of your notes and readings. Not only are these great to study from in the days leading up to the exam, but the act of preparing them helps you break down the material, group things together, ingrain them in your memory, and fill gaps in your knowledge. Your study sheet can be one or several pages, but it should be short enough to read in a single sitting.

The type of review sheet you create depends on the class and the type of exam, but here are some general guidelines. For STEM classes, it should contain formulas, key terms, and examples of the major types of problems you've seen in class and homework. For humanities classes, it should include major themes as well as key dates, names, and terms. If the test will include questions about different readings, it should list the texts, the authors, and the main points of each.

In Their Own Words

"Writing or typing out summaries from textbooks or class notes...helped me process it so I could reproduce the concepts or facts on a test."

—Rhodes Scholar and valedictorian in high school and college

"Take notes when studying for a test. Even if you don't look back at them, the act of taking notes is quite helpful."

—College valedictorian

Review Sheet Samples

Here's an excerpt from a review sheet I created for a college class called Literature Humanities. Since the test was going to consist of a couple of essay questions about the books we had read, I wanted to be really clear on the Big Ideas—so I went through my class notes and identified the major themes of each text.

Ovid (*The Art of Love*)

- Life as a spectacle, a play, art; making art out of life.
- Reading as a seduction.
- The primacy of individual interests.
- Turning love or passion into art; the rationalization of the irrational.

Boccaccio (*The Decameron*)

- Compassion, pity are infectious.
- Human truth vs. absolute truth.
- Culture facilitates sexuality.

- The instability of language.
- Words create their own reality; equating the figurative with the literal.

Montaigne (*Essays*)

- Faith and reason are not compatible.
- Disjunction between body and mind.
- We can know ourselves only through artifice or culture.
- Change is the only constant.

The review sheet made it much easier to compare and contrast the texts and predict potential essay questions. For example, I noticed that the nature of language and the struggle between nature and culture kept showing up again and again—so I made sure I had some good examples of these themes ready to go for the exam.

Review sheets are especially handy when it comes to foreign languages. All those conjugations and grammar rules can really add up, and having them in one place helps you notice subtle but important details. You should also include plenty of examples so you'll remember how to use these rules months or even years from now. Here's an excerpt of a review sheet I created for German—or, as Mark Twain called it, "The Awful German Language."

Definite Articles (the)			
	Masc.	**Fem.**	**Neuter**	**Plural**
Nominative	der	die	das	die
Genitive	des	der	des	der
Dative	dem	der	dem	den
Accusative	den	die	das	die

(These are all different ways of saying "the" in German. The cases—nominative, genitive, etc.—indicate the word's grammatical function in the sentence.)

Possessive Adjectives:
mein (my), *dein* (your), *sein* (his, its), *ihr/Ihr* (her, their/your), *unser* (our), *euer* (your)

Comparative: ends in *–er(–)*.

Superlative: ends in *–st(–)*.
Or use "*am* […] *–sten*" (example: *am kleinsten* = the smallest)

(Here I give some examples of verb tenses and conjugations.)

Present Tense Example:
machen (to do):

ich mache (I do)	*wir machen* (we do)
du machst (you do)	*ihr macht* (you do)
Sie machen (you do)	*Sie machen* (you do)
er macht (he does)	*sie machen* (they do)
sie macht (she does)	
es macht (it does)	
man macht (people do)	

Preterite Example: take stem, add *–te*
machen:

ich machte (I did)	*wir machten* (we did)
du machtest (you did)	*ihr machtet* (you did)
man machte (people did)	*sie machten* (they did)

Future Tense: *werden* + infinitive (or present tense with future implied).
Example: *ich werde…machen* (I will do)

Passive Voice: *werden* + past participle.

Example: *ich werde…gesehen* (I am seen)

Three Game-Changing Learning Techniques: Self-Testing, Interleaving, and Spacing

People who study learning for a living have long known about these grade-boosting methods, but many students still haven't heard about them. Here's how you can incorporate these scientifically proven strategies into your studying.

The Importance of Self-Testing

I know what you're thinking—"I get enough tests in class. Now I've got to do them at home, too?" But quizzing yourself is easier than you may think, and research shows it's one of the best ways to learn. In a 2006 study by Washington University in St. Louis, students who were tested repeatedly on a reading passage remembered more than 60 percent of it one week later, compared with 40 percent remembered by a group that had only read it a couple of times. This was despite the fact that the latter felt more confident about their retention of the material.[74]

A Kent State study has shown that students retain foreign vocabulary better when they're asked to recall the meaning of words rather than study them side by side.[75] And in a recent survey of 324 undergrads, researchers confirmed that self-testing is significantly associated with higher GPA.[76] Quizzing yourself is a more powerful and efficient method than reading the material over and over and over again—so although it takes a little planning and initiative, you'll actually save time and retain more in the end.

So how can you make self-testing part of your everyday study routine? For starters, if you're given a practice test with solutions, do the questions by yourself before looking at the answers. Similarly, when studying flash cards and lists, don't look at the answers until you've tried coming up with them on your own.

You should also quiz yourself on the readings. You can often find ready-to-use questions at the end of textbook chapters. If these aren't available, try making questions out of the headings of each section. However, don't just glance at the questions and say, "Yeah, I could answer that." For best results, write down your answers on a piece of paper or say them out loud.

In Their Own Words

"Make a mock exam the day before the real exam. Use old exams or write questions that you think will be on the exam. Then close your notes and give yourself the same amount of time as the real exam and answer all the questions. Finally, review your mock exam and correct any wrong questions. An exam is just [like] a performance in a sport or theater, so it is silly to approach it without practice."

—Rhodes Scholar and Goldwater Scholar

Variety Is the Spice of Life—and Learning.

Switching between distinct but related tasks during a study session, instead of focusing on one thing the entire time, can do wonders for your comprehension. (Learning experts call this "interleaving.") For example, if you're studying a little *español*, don't just memorize vocabulary words for hours on end—mix it up with reading a story in Spanish, listening to a language CD, and reviewing grammar.

Why does interleaving work? Because it forces your brain to make connections between things: you have to compare concepts, figure out when to apply one method and not another, and put what you learned into practice. Perhaps just as importantly, switching between topics makes studying *less boring!* It's like when you go to the gym—would you rather spend the whole time doing stomach crunches, or taking turns between that and push-ups, jumping jacks, and running on the treadmill?

The Secret of Spacing

Simply put, spacing is the opposite of cramming, and it's a powerful tool for getting better grades. According to learning experts, recall and comprehension improve when you spread out your studying rather than lump it all together.[77] In other words, it's better to study an hour tonight, an hour on the weekend, and an hour a week from now than to study something for three hours in a row. You're not putting in more time or effort; you're just getting more out of it.

Pretty cool, huh? No one's quite sure why spacing works, but it could be because it forces you to recall what you've learned, compare it to what you're learning now, and pinpoint and correct misunderstandings. If you study everything in one go (called "massing"), you don't have that opportunity.

When you study, try making several passes over the material, leaving a few days between each pass. You'll find that each time you'll absorb a little more, make more connections, and see the big picture more clearly. For the first pass, skim the material to prep your brain for what's coming. Next, read things slowly and carefully. At this stage you may feel like you're not accomplishing much, but when you look at the text again, you may be surprised by how much clearer it's become. Your passes through the material will get faster and more productive as time goes on.

> The learning process involves taking things apart—examining each concept by itself—and then putting them back together—synthesizing these concepts and understanding them as parts of a whole. You can't do this all in one sitting; real learning takes time.

Spacing and Interleaving: An Unbeatable Pair

Spacing and interleaving are even more effective when used together. This isn't hard to do, since interleaving naturally spaces out your review of a topic. Let's say you're learning four new things—A, B, C, and D—which can be distinct but related topics in any area. So, by applying spacing *and* interleaving, your study sessions should look something like this:

ABCD CABD BADC CBDA

As you can see, your review of each topic is spaced out because you're interleaving it with the other three. Note that it's better to mix things up than to do them in the same order every time (ABCD ABCD ABCD ABCD), so you don't get the right answer simply by predicting what's next.

To make spacing and interleaving part of your everyday study habits, have a strategy for every test. Before you start preparing, think about how you can break up the material into distinct but related topics, and alternate between them as you study. For STEM classes, do practice problems out of order. Let's say your math teacher tells you to do ten questions from Chapter 1 and another ten from Chapter 2 for homework. Instead of answering them sequentially, alternate between questions from the first and second chapters. This forces you to think about which rules and formulas you have to apply. Just make sure everything's in order when you hand in the assignment!

One of the most important applications of these learning techniques is to *start early and space it out*. Study every subject a little at a time rather than condensing it into one massive review session. This is another way of

> ### Survey Says
>
> Most top students realize the value of spreading things out. In high school, the plurality (31 percent) said that they rarely crammed for exams, and 20 percent said they never did. In college, 38 percent report rarely cramming, and 16 percent still avoided it completely.

saying, "*Do not cram!*" Cramming leads to very poor retention of material—what you study will be in your head one day, out the next.

In Their Own Words

When asked about their studying strategies, many top students described their own homegrown varieties of spacing and interleaving:

"I found it most effective to study a little bit every day for every class I was enrolled in, rather than studying for long blocks of time once or twice a week. Repetition is key to absorbing new material. If you study every day, by the time the test comes around you will feel prepared without the stress that comes from cramming."

—Winner of Best in Category, Intel Science Fair

"Study a little bit each day and make sure you are meeting your milestones."

—National Spelling Bee champion

"Despite my always doing it, last-minute studying was never of value. If there are things that need to be memorized, start working on that early."

—College valedictorian

"Start studying early; read through notes often. Don't study the same subject for too long (switch it up). Set a plan at the beginning of the week for what you will study and when."

—Rhodes Scholar and 2010 NCAA Woman of the Year

"Make a plan about the order and distribution of time across subjects. Use different techniques and mix it up."

—Rhodes Scholar and winner of the ESPN
Academic All-American Division I award

How to Become a Master of Memorization

Memorization has gotten a bad rap recently. Lots of students, and even some educators, say that being able to reason is more important than knowing facts; and besides, why bother committing things to memory when you've got Google? My response to this—after I've finished inwardly groaning—is that of course reasoning is important, but that doesn't mean you shouldn't know facts as well. It's not like you have to choose between one or the other. Besides, facts give you a foundation on which to reason about things.

As for depending on Google, it's hard to have an intelligent conversation if you have to look something up every ten seconds. And it's never good to be reliant on external devices—what if you can't access the Internet, or you lose your iPhone, or your battery dies? Whether you agree with this or not, most teachers still require you to know things by heart. The following are some active learning techniques that'll make you a master memorizer.

Flash Card Facts

Flash cards are a cheap and easy way of learning material. You can take them wherever you go and study as much or as little as you want; you can shuffle them up and group them into stacks; you can test yourself or have a friend quiz you. But believe it or not, there's been a lot of research on this seemingly simple method of studying.

One of the findings from this research is that *it's better to use one large stack than several smaller ones*. This goes back to the theory of spacing: the bigger your stack, the greater the space between items. Take, for example, a 2009 study in which students who reviewed vocab from a stack of twenty flash cards had much better recall than those who studied the same words in four stacks of five cards each.[78]

You should also *think twice before dropping a card from your stack*, even if you feel like you know it. In a 2008 experiment by Nate

Kornell and Robert Bjork, one group of students was allowed to set aside flash cards they thought they knew, while the others had to leave the deck intact. When they were tested on the material—a list of Swahili words—immediately afterward and a week later, the no-drop group scored significantly better.[79]

This might seem to go against common sense. After all, the more easy items you remove, the more you'll get to review the ones giving you trouble, right? But as with many things, it's not that simple. You may know that *wingu* means "cloud" in Swahili, but leaving it in your deck will help you retain that knowledge. Plus, as we saw above, it's better to study from a large stack than a small one—and the more cards you take away, the punier your stack becomes.

If you want to get fancy with your flash cards, use something called *the Leitner system*. In this method, which is based on the theory of spaced repetition, you have several stacks or boxes of flash cards. Let's keep it simple and say you have three boxes. The first box, which you review the most often (say once a day), contains items you got wrong or haven't seen before. When you get one of these cards right, you put it in the second box, which you review less often (every other day).

When you get a card from the second box right, you put it into the third box, which you review even less often (maybe every four days). Whenever you get something wrong from boxes 2 or 3, you put it back in the first box. That way, you review the ones you have trouble with more often, and you never stop reviewing any of the cards.

Don't want to worry about when to study what, or where to store all those boxes? No problem! Download a free electronic flash-card program such as Anki (http://ankisrs.net/) or the Mnemosyne Project (http://www.mnemosyne-proj.org/). Just type in what you want to memorize and let the software do the rest.

Give Lists Some Love

Beware of spending so long making flash cards that you don't have enough time to review them! When days are short and your list is long, don't bother rewriting every item on a 3x5-inch piece of paper. If the material's already in one convenient place—for example, at the end of a chapter, in the back of the book, on the Internet, or in a handout your teacher gave you—just study directly from the source. To test yourself, simply cover up the answer column with your hand. If you get something wrong, make a mark next to it in pencil so you can come back to it later. And don't forget to test yourself in both directions. If you're studying Spanish vocab, make sure you can go from English to Spanish as well as Spanish to English.

One problem with studying from lists, however, is that people tend to remember the beginning and the end better than the middle. (This is known as the serial position effect.) A simple way to prevent this is to start reviewing from a different place each time. Studying from a list can also make it difficult to identify terms out of order, so it's a good idea to pick items from the list at random when you're testing yourself.

> Here's a creative way to memorize things: make a list, laminate it or cover it in Saran wrap, and tape it to the wall of your shower. Get clean and smart at the same time!

When in Doubt, Write It Out

You know how in the opening credits of *The Simpsons*, Bart is always writing something twenty times on the blackboard? Things like, "The capital of Montana is not 'Hannah'" and "I will not eat things for money"? Well, this may be Bart's everlasting punishment, but it's also an excellent way to burn things into your brain.

Grab a pad of paper and write out things like Spanish verb tenses, physics formulas, and the dates of Revolutionary War battles. Write each item ten to twenty times per sitting, until you feel like you could conjugate the first-person preterite of *hablar* in your sleep.

Note: Do *not* just copy things from a book as you write; you should be actively recalling them from memory to get the best results.

Say It Loud, Say It Proud...Sometimes

In a 2010 study, people who read half a list of words silently and spoke the other half recalled the spoken words much better than the silent ones. In other words, saying things out loud seemed to help them remember it.[80] So does this mean you should stand up in the middle of the library and give an impromptu reading of *The Fundamentals of Calculus*? Fortunately for your fellow students, the answer is no. It turns out that this memory boost occurs only when you read things out loud *once in a while*, not when you do it all the time.

Test subjects who verbalized the whole list of words remembered them no better than a group who read the entire list silently. If you start saying everything out loud, it's no longer a distinctive, memorable event. So save your breath for the really important stuff that's more likely to show up on tests—key terms, formulas, big ideas, and so on. By the way, if you're in public and don't want people to think you're crazy, you can get the same benefit from silently mouthing the words.

Mnemonic Devices

Please Excuse My Dear Aunt Sally, My Very Energetic Mother Just Served Us Nine Pizzas (although the Pizzas have since disappeared!), Roy G. Biv—do these sound familiar to you? You probably learned lots of mnemonic devices as a kid, and what's more, you probably still remember them.

Rhymes, acronyms, mental images, silly phrases, and memorable word groupings are great ways to learn material at any age, and you don't have to wait for somebody to make them up for you. If you're drawing a blank, grab a dictionary and pick a word based on the first letter of each term you're trying to remember, or plug them into one of these handy mnemonic generators:

- http://spacefem.com/mnemonics/
- http://human-factors.arc.nasa.gov/cognition/tutorials/mnemonics/index.html (The Mnemonicizer, from the people who brought you the Space Shuttle!)

Train Your Brain (On the Train)

If you take public transportation, this is an excellent time to stretch out those synapses. There's something about the way the wheels on the bus go round and round, or the steady hum of the engine, that primes the brain for memorization. While it may not be the best time to study, say, multivariate calculus, commuting is great for relatively straightforward tasks like reviewing outlines, lists, flash cards, or the glossaries at the back of your books. If you get jostled around a lot, use spiral-bound index cards instead of the loose ones so your stuff doesn't go flying.

Is There Such a Thing as Over-Studying?

Not really. While a lot of students won't look at a topic once they feel like they know it, a really good student will keep going until he or she has got it practically by heart. (Cognitive psychologists call this over-learning.) In the heat of an exam, it's not just about whether you know something, it's also about how fast you can recall it. If you have to keep dredging things out of your memory like a stick out of mud, you may not have time to finish the test or check your answers. Plus, it's much easier to blank out on things you only know superficially. Overlearning makes coming up with the right answer practically effortless.

While there's no such thing as over-studying, there *is* such a thing as spending too much time on one thing and not enough time on something else. If you have a lot of topics to cover, make sure you devote enough time to each. Interleaving will help you avoid this problem.

> **Don't slack off too much after midterms.** I know it can be tempting—it's spring, the weather's getting warm, and you've just survived a grueling round of exams. But this is the perfect time to get ahead of your classmates. By studying in this lull between midterms and finals, when everyone else is taking it relatively easy, you'll be at a big advantage by the end of the semester.

How to Study Something You Hate

It happens to all of us sooner or later—we find ourselves in a class so painful that it makes a root canal look like a walk in the park. You have no interest in it. It's hard, it's boring, and the mere sight of a book on the subject makes you want to run the other way. So how do you make it through this term of torture?

Try *bargaining with yourself*. If you can't bear the thought of reading a chapter in depth, say that you'll skim it for now. When you go back to it later, it'll be easier to digest. Can't imagine devoting a whole hour to this detestable subject? Commit to ten or twenty minutes—a little is better than nothing at all. And when you get to the end of that time, you might find yourself saying, "Hey, this isn't as bad as I thought. Maybe I could go for a *few* more minutes."

You should also *make yourself extra comfortable* when it's time to study your least-favorite subject. Go to your best study spot, put on some relaxing music, maybe take a shower before you crack open the book. Try to study when you're most relaxed. You should be awake enough to concentrate, but not so awake that you're too restless to read something incredibly dry and boring. I find the best times for this are shortly after waking up and a little before I go to bed.

And don't forget to *reward yourself*. You know the deal—eat some chocolate, check Facebook, go for a walk, watch TV, chat with a friend. Give yourself something to look forward to after struggling through an assignment.

When studying a subject you hate, make sure you *know what the purpose is*. It might not always be obvious, but it is there. If you're a high school student with dreams of becoming an English major, you may wonder why you have to suffer through pre-calculus. Keep reminding yourself that it's bringing you one step closer to your goal of getting *into* college. Universities want to see advanced coursework in a variety of subjects, not just the one you plan to specialize in. Besides, lots of people change their plans. What if you decide to get a BA in English *and* do pre-med? You'll be glad you stuck it out with pre-calc.

Physical Tips for Studying

You may think that studying's all in the mind, but it's got a physical side as well. The right environment can do wonders for your concentration. You should be comfortable when you study, because you're going to be doing a lot of it! If you're constantly thinking about the lighting or the temperature or your aching back, you might not give your work the attention it deserves. Here's how to make studying a more pleasant experience.

Where Should You Study?

Everyone knows you should study in a quiet, well-lit place with few distractions. But where should this place be? At home, in the library, in the student lounge?

Research shows that you may be better off alternating where you study. In a 1978 experiment by Robert Bjork and others, college students were given a list of forty words to memorize. One group reviewed the list in two different rooms, while the others spent all their time in a single location. When they were tested on the vocab, the nomads recalled an average of 24.4 words, compared to 15.9 by the stationary group.[81]

Being in different environments seems to enrich the information that's being stored in your brain, making it stay there longer. So consider staking out a number of learning zones—the rooms in your house, the library, a quiet café, a student lounge, a park— and switching locations every few hours or going to a different place each day. Remember that all of your study spots should be relatively quiet and distraction-free. If you have after-school access to the room where the test's being given, you may be in luck. Researchers have found that students perform even better when they take exams in the same environment as where they studied.[82]

Survey Says

Home is the most popular place for studying among top students. Of that group, 50 percent say they do their best studying there, while 30 percent prefer the library. Only 9 percent favor holing up in a coffee shop. Your room is typically the best place for controlling your environment, finding your comfort zone, and enjoying a little peace and quiet. However, some people just can't resist temptations like TV, video games, bed, and the Internet. Others have roommates whose obnoxious habits drive them up the wall. If your room is a den of distractions rather than a fortress of solitude, it might be time to hightail it to the nearest library.

In Their Own Words

"I like to rotate [studying] between home, library, and coffee shops. It also depends on the type of work."

—Rhodes Scholar and Goldwater Scholar

When Should You Study?

The fact of the matter is, when you're a busy high school or college student, you've got to study whenever you can. However, research shows that some times are better for learning than others. *Studying in the afternoon or evening* seems to have the best effect on long-term memory, even for those who say they're morning people.[83]

Researchers have also found that *learning something shortly before bedtime will help you retain it.* In a 2012 University of Notre Dame study, for example, test subjects recalled a list of word pairs better when they went to sleep soon after studying than when they learned it early in the day.[84] So try memorizing things like facts, dates, and formulas before calling it a night. This has the added benefit of making it a cinch to fall asleep!

Don't Be a Hothead

Make sure your study space is on the cool side *and* has good ventilation. In 2004 and 2005, researchers found that students performed better on exercises when the temperature was lowered from 77 degrees to 68 degrees, and when the air supply rate was increased. Although the number of errors they made didn't change significantly, they did get the exercises done faster.[85]

Nature Knows Best

Did you know that going green is good for the environment *and* your grades? It's true—you can increase your productivity simply by adding plants to your work space. In a 2010 study, test subjects performed several demanding cognitive tasks in an office setting with four indoor plants, while another group did the same tasks in a room minus the greenery. The result: the plant people's performance improved after completing the first task, but the other group's did not.[86]

No one's quite sure why plants have this effect on people. It could be because of the oxygen they produce, or maybe the presence of nature helps people relax and focus, or perhaps it's a combination of the two. Whatever the case, get yourself down to the plant store and pick up a few hardy specimens.

If you're in a classroom where there isn't any greenery, try to sit by the window—just having a view of the great outdoors can improve performance. And if you live in a house with a backyard, or if your campus is a landscaped wonderland of green meadows and rolling hills, this is the perfect opportunity to study outside. Natural light, fresh air, and plants are all excellent study aids.

Gimme a Break

Think of your brain as a muscle. You wouldn't go to the gym and work out for hours without taking a breather, would you? Well, you shouldn't shut yourself up in a room and study that way, either. There's no question that breaks help prevent burnout. In a 2011 study by psychologist Alejandro Lleras, for example, test subjects who worked nonstop on a computerized task for fifty minutes showed a decline in performance, while those who took two brief breaks were as attentive at the end of the task as they were in the beginning.[87]

> **Survey Says**
>
> Top students are big fans of taking breaks. The plurality (41 percent) went on break about once an hour; 18 percent said they took breaks whenever they felt like it; 16 percent said about once every two hours; and 11 percent more than once an hour. What do they do during these breaks? All kinds of things: checked email, took naps, talked to friends, exercised, took a bathroom break, watched TV, and so on.

Although you shouldn't force yourself to stop working if you're in the zone, doing something else when your mind starts to drift will help you get back on track. Breaks are also useful because you remember the first and last things you study better than the stuff in the middle. The more breaks you take, the more firsts and lasts you'll have stored in your memory.

> Instead of forcing yourself to do marathon cramming sessions, study in a series of twenty- or thirty-minute bursts broken up by short (five-minute or less) breaks. Even resting for a minute or two can help keep you fresh and focused.

Get Moving!

Can't stop fidgeting when you study? Does the thought of sitting quietly in the library for hours make you go off the deep end? Well, take heart! There's no law that says you have to sit still to learn. If you have access to a treadmill, grab a book and take a nice, long stroll as you read—or just walk around your room while you're holding the book. (Make sure you get rid of all obstructions first.) Squeeze a stress ball or chew some gum to relieve tension while you're stuck in the classroom.

Recruit Your Pet as a Study Partner

Cats are usually more than happy to do this—in fact, you may have trouble keeping them off keyboards and books—and dogs will often serve as well. Few things are more relaxing than having a warm, furry creature next to you as you study.

A Soundtrack for Studying?

In the early '90s, Mozart CDs flew off the shelf as news came out that listening to this classical composer could raise your IQ. Unfortunately, later studies revealed that playing *Eine kleine Nachtmusik* would *not* turn you into a genius—but that doesn't mean Mozart has no impact on your brain. The real effects of his music are much more subtle and complex.

Let's take a look at a 1999 experiment by Kristin Nantais and E. Glenn Schellenberg in which test subjects performed spatial reasoning tasks after hearing a piece by Mozart, listening to a Stephen King story, or sitting in silence.[88] The result: the people who preferred Mozart did better after listening to the music; the ones who preferred the story did better after hearing the King tale; and both groups outperformed the ones sitting in silence. (It's worth noting, though, that the people who preferred Mozart did the best overall.)

What seems to be happening here is a psychological phenomenon known as arousal—and no, I'm not talking about anything dirty! In this case, arousal is a measure of mental stimulation. Too little arousal, and people are bored and unmotivated; too much, and they're stressed out and anxious. Get it just right, and their performance skyrockets. When you like something—such as music or a story—your mood and concentration tend to improve, which in turn can raise your score on cognitive tests. So as it turns out, Mozart may give your brain a boost after all—but only if you *like* Mozart.

And lots of people *do* like Mozart, especially when they're studying. It's calming, it's not too distracting, and it puts you in a studious frame of mind. Perhaps more importantly, you can use it to block out annoying background noise. I have a playlist of "study music" ready to go on my iPod, and it's a lifesaver when I have to read in a public place. It also comes in handy when I'm by myself and things

> ## Survey Says
> Top students are fairly evenly split on this issue: 48 percent say they listen to music when they study, while 52 percent say they don't. However, most high achievers (54 percent) believe that they concentrate better with the sound of silence. Of the rest, 34 percent say music helps them focus, and 12 percent feel it makes no difference. The bottom line is: do what works best for you. If tunes are a distraction, then study in peace and quiet; but if the silence is driving you crazy, give the music mentioned here a try.

are a *bit* too quiet. I don't only listen to Mozart, however; I also play Bach, Boccherini, Vivaldi, Schubert, and many others. My favorite pieces for studying are Mozart's violin concertos, which I've listened to nearly every day since junior high school! Whether or not Mozart has improved my IQ, it does wonders for my concentration.

You don't have to limit yourself to Mozart or classical, but there are some general rules to follow when choosing a study soundtrack. The music should fade into the background, not demand your attention. Make sure it's *instrumental only*, as lyrics interfere with learning. You use the same part of your brain for studying as you do for listening to music with words. That means that Jay-Z, Lady Gaga, and Beyoncé are out.

Not all classical music is the same. A lot of people use the word "classical" to refer to any music that's old and European, but these tunes actually fall into several distinct periods, including Baroque, Classical with a big C, Romantic, and Modern. Baroque is the earliest and includes composers like Bach, Vivaldi, and Handel. The man at the center of the controversy—Wolfgang Amadeus Mozart—belongs to the Classical age. Next comes the Romantic period, and as you can tell from the name, its music is passionate and emotional. Composers like Beethoven (in the later part of his career), Wagner, Liszt, and Chopin take center stage here. While Baroque and Classical music tends to have steady rhythm and pleasant melodies, without being too loud or too soft, pieces from the Romantic period and beyond are generally much more variable and distracting. (As much as I love Beethoven, I simply can't concentrate with *Ode to Joy* playing in the background.) Later composers did some amazing things, but creating the perfect piece of study music was not one of them.

Study music should have a steady rhythm and a relatively constant volume. And it should be upbeat rather than sad or angry, since songs that produce positive emotions are more likely to help you learn. In a 2001 experiment by William Thompson, E. Glenn Schellenberg, and Gabriela Husain, test subjects who listened to a lively Mozart sonata did better on a spatial reasoning task than those who heard a sad adagio by the composer Albinoni.[89] If you don't like classical, some other likely candidates are *smooth jazz, electronic music, and movie soundtracks.*

Researchers have found that **making music** may be the real key to raising your IQ. According to Lutz Jäncke, a psychologist at the University of Zurich, learning an instrument can increase IQ by several points.[90] Although the effects are more pronounced in those who start playing as children, making music at any age can boost the parts of the brain that process patterns, understand language, and control memory. So if you already know how to play an instrument, keep practicing; and if you've never made music before, it's not too late to start. Consider buying a cheap keyboard and learning to play some melodies with a "teach-yourself-piano" book. Playing as little as an hour a week for several months can literally fine-tune your brain.

Study Groups: Join with Caution

Lots of people, including some education experts, will tell you that study groups are the way to go. They can make studying more fun, help students stay motivated, and give them the opportunity to learn from one another. And this is all true—*up to a point*. While study groups can be good in certain situations (which we'll discuss later), they have many hidden dangers—such as leading you to rely on others for explanation and motivation when these things should really come from inside yourself.

The social aspect can make it difficult to concentrate and think critically. Seeing somebody working on a different but related task can actually slow you down, according to a 2007 University of Calgary study by Tim Welsh.[91] Perhaps even more troubling, people in study groups may give you wrong information. Your classmates probably don't know more and may even know less than you, so all too often it becomes a case of the blind leading the blind. You might be better off getting help from the real experts: your textbook, your TA (if you have one), and your teacher.

> **Survey Says**
>
> Most top students are not big fans of study groups. About 57 percent said they joined them only "a few times," while over 20 percent said they never joined one. Of those who did participate in study groups, most said it helped them only a little (53 percent) or not at all (19 percent). Social studying can help with basic understanding of a subject, but to take it to the next level, you may have to go it alone.

In their report "Improving Undergraduate Learning: Findings and Policy Recommendations from the SSRC-CLA Longitudinal Project," Richard Arum, Josipa Roksa, and Esther Cho found that spending more hours studying alone is associated with improvement in critical thinking, complex reasoning, and written communication skills among college students.[92]

With that said, there are plenty of situations where it *is* smart to join the crowd. For example:

- You have a problem staying focused, and working with others helps keep you on track. Think of it as AA for procrastinators.
- You're an aural learner—that is, you learn best by listening.

- You want to practice conversation for a language class.
- The other people in the group really know their stuff, and there's a lot you can learn from them.
- You can't go to a teacher or TA for help.
- You've finished studying all the required material and want to test your knowledge with others.
- You want to go over exercises for a class, and group discussion is allowed. (Make sure you know your teacher's policy on this, because the last thing you want is to be accused of cheating.)

And if you do join a study group, make sure you follow these six simple rules:

1. **Don't let the group get too big**. Things might get out of control with more than six or seven people.
2. Stay away from groups that use studying as an excuse to PARTAAAY!
3. **Don't hesitate to ask a question**, give your opinion, or help someone who's having trouble.
4. **Choose someone to be "the leader"** to keep the group on track, or take turns if no one wants this role for the entire semester.
5. **Don't split up homework assignments among members of the group**. It's much harder to learn the material if you don't do all the questions—and besides, how do you know something's done right if you don't do it yourself?
6. **Have a specific goal for each meeting**. What are you trying to accomplish—is it working on homework problems, trying to understand a concept, or discussing a chapter in a book?

In Their Own Words

"Do all the homework. In college, a lot of students would do problem sets in groups, each student taking a couple of problems, and then sharing answers. I never did this; I worked through each problem myself and didn't check against anyone. This forced me to think through every problem in detail, and gave me more thorough practice, even if I got some of them wrong."

—Top student and graduate of Carnegie Mellon University

"Coordinate with friends to study quietly together and then take breaks together."

—Yale Law School student

How Much Is Enough?

So far we've been discussing *how* to study, but now let's turn our attention to the equally important but often overlooked question of *how much* to study. (In this context, studying refers to reading, doing homework, and any other preparation for a subject outside of class time; doing a math problem or reading an assigned text counts just as much as cramming for an exam the following day.) You may be wondering what a "normal" amount of study time is for American students. There's no one answer, since it varies from school to school, region to region, grade to grade, and so on, but here's some info to give you an idea.

High school:
- 63 percent of high school sophomores spend ten hours or less a week on homework.[93]
- Most high school students spend five hours or less a week reading or studying for class.[94]

College:

- 65 percent of college freshmen and 56 percent of college seniors spend ten hours or less per week studying and doing homework.[95]
- The average full-time college student spends between twelve and fourteen hours per week studying, which is about 50 percent less time than several decades ago.[96]

Now take a look at the statistics for the top students I surveyed:

Survey says

High school:

- 20 percent spent fewer than 10 hours a week studying and doing homework.
- 50 percent spent between 10 and 20 hours a week.
- 30 percent spent 20 hours or more. Of this 30 percent, 20 percent spent between 20 and 30 hours, and 10 percent more than 30 hours.

College:

- 4 percent spent 10 hours or less a week studying and doing homework.
- 29 percent spent between 11 and 20 hours a week.
- 42 percent spent between 20 and 30 hours.
- 25 percent spent more than 30 hours.

Take a look at this chart comparing how much time typical college seniors and the top students in my survey (as undergrads) spend studying and doing homework per week. (The stats for the former come from a 2009 survey of over 24,000 graduating seniors.)[97] The results are rather jarring.

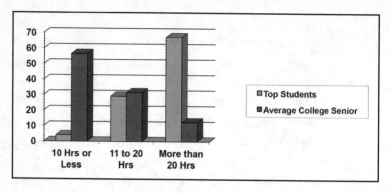

As you can see, the top students study *a lot* more than their peers. While many people in high school and college prepare for ten hours or less a week, only 20 percent of the high achievers did that in high school, and *almost none* did so in college. The majority studied more than 20 hours per week as undergrads, and almost everyone in this group said that hard work played a major role in their success. When asked to rate the importance of hard work on a scale of 1 to 10, 43 percent of the top students gave it a perfect 10, and 27 percent gave it a 9; this was second only to determination.

> **Study time** for college students has dropped from about twenty-four hours per week in 1961 to fourteen hours in 2003, according to a report by Babcock and Marks.[98] That's a loss of approximately 300 hours or 12.5 days of studying per school year!

The Global Classroom

Let's look at the issue from a broader perspective. In case you've been living under a rock for the last few years, you know that students in many Asian countries have been kicking our butts. For example, in the 2009 PISA (Program for International Student Assessment) test of high school students in sixty-five countries and regions, the

United States came in twenty-third in science, seventeenth in reading, and thirty-first in math.

The real winners were the nations or regions of Shanghai, China; Hong Kong, China; Singapore; Japan; Korea; Taiwan; and, making a surprise appearance, the Scandinavian country of Finland. Take a look at the chart to see where each one came in. Arne Duncan, U.S. Secretary of Education, called the results "an absolute wake-up call for America." If the U.S. is to remain competitive in the global economy, its students must catch up to their foreign peers.

Results of the 2009 PISA Test		
Science	**Math**	**Reading**
Shanghai, China	Shanghai, China	Shanghai, China
Finland	Singapore	Korea
Hong Kong, China	Hong Kong, China	Finland
Singapore	Korea	Hong Kong, China
Japan	Taiwan	Singapore
Korea	Finland	Canada
…	…	…
United States (23)	United States (31)	United States (17)

Source: PISA 2009 at a Glance, *OECD Publishing (2010),* http://dx.doi.org/10.1787/9789264095298-en.

There are a lot of possible reasons for Asia's success. It's been attributed to cultural values, better teachers, a stronger work ethic, longer school days, shorter summer vacations, parental pressure, fiercer competition for university spots and jobs, and many other factors. In his book *Outliers*, Malcolm Gladwell even links it to the labor-intensive rice-paddy economy of southern Asia.[99] Probably all of these things play a role, but I want to talk about the ones *you* have control over. Let's look at some stats about Asian—specifically Chinese—students. As you'll see, it's not just top American students who are putting in the extra time.

- Chinese students spend twice as many hours doing homework as their peers in the United States.[100]
- According to one survey, Chinese high school students study for an average of seventeen hours per week.[101]

The average Chinese student seems to study a lot more like a top student than the average American scholar. *Time* magazine put it bluntly in the article "Five Things the U.S. Can Learn from China" when it stated, "The Chinese understand that there is no substitute for putting in the hours and doing the work."[102] According to the Asia Society's 2005 report on education in China, "Effort, not ability, is presumed to determine success in school."[103] In other words, *what matters isn't how naturally talented you are, but how hard you try.* This is an important part of the Chinese attitude toward education, and it's something you can apply to your own life no matter where you come from. By contrast, many American students fail to see the connection between hard work and success.[104]

There's no "magic number" of hours you have to study to succeed in school, but many college professors recommend two hours of studying per every hour of class time. So according to this rule, if you're taking five three-credit courses—where a credit represents an hour of class time—you should be studying about thirty hours a week ((3 x 2) x 5). If you're in high school, you might want to consider each of your classes to be a two- or three-credit course.

However, I find this view a little simplistic. There are too many variables such as the difficulty of each class, how reading-intensive it is, and how fast you work. I've had some three-credit classes where I barely had to work at all and others which ate up nearly half my overall study time. But the rule does give you a rough idea of how much you should be doing. Not surprisingly, there's a direct connection between how much you study and your grades. Decreasing study time by about forty minutes per day lowers GPA by an average of 0.24 points.[105]

Keep in mind that I am *not* telling you to become a hermit, locking yourself away in your room after class and memorizing your textbook. But studying ten to twenty hours a week, or even twenty to thirty hours, doesn't seem excessive, especially when you consider that you can make up a lot of time on the weekends. If you study or do homework for two hours a day after school, you've got ten right there. Add in a few hours over the weekend, and you're well on your way to twenty.

Consider devoting half your weekend to your schoolwork and the other half to whatever you want to do. The weekend is prime study time, since you've (hopefully) caught up on your sleep and won't have as many distractions from classes and friends. Your parents—people with regular jobs—may get evenings and weekends off, but don't try to copy their lifestyle. The sooner you accept that you'll often have to work while the adults get playtime, the better.

> ## Survey Says
>
> The vast majority (79 percent) of the top students I surveyed said that their achievements came at a price. When asked to describe the kind of sacrifices they made, their answers sound remarkably similar:
>
> "Personal time, social events"
>
> "Social life, time, sleep"
>
> "Less time socializing/ having fun."
>
> "Less social time spent studying with friends...Less time spent in pursuit of sports."
>
> "Time spent with friends."
>
> "Less free time than many of my friends..."
>
> "Limited social life."
>
> "Didn't go out with friends as often..."
>
> "Devoted more time to course work than to social life"
>
> "Socializing in general..."
>
> "Less social activity..."

Some people may be horrified by the idea of downsizing their social life, but the amount of socializing that goes on in high schools and colleges seems to be spiraling out of control. In a study examining why up to 45 percent of U.S. college students fail to improve in core academic skills—you know, just little things like critical thinking, writing, and reasoning—Arum and Roksa say that this is partly due to students' "defin[ing] and understand[ing] their college experiences as being focused more on social than on academic development." Students spend about one-third of their all-too-few study hours with their peers, an arrangement which is "not generally conducive to learning."[106]

Being able to work by yourself is a skill that's often overlooked, but solitude fosters independence, concentration, creativity, and original thinking. And socializing isn't the only thing U.S. students are doing too much of: according to a 2010 report by the Kaiser Family Foundation, Americans age eighteen and younger spend an average of seven hours and thirty-eight minutes *a day* using entertainment media.[107] If students are able to devote nearly half their waking hours to watching TV, listening to music, playing video games, sending texts, and surfing the Web, they have little excuse for not hitting the books more.

Some students say they're too busy with jobs or extracurriculars to devote more time to their studies. It *is* important to do stuff outside of school, both for your sanity and for your resumé. But you should also ask yourself whether you've bitten off more than you can chew. It's no secret that students have become chronically overscheduled, jumping from activity to activity, often at the expense of their schoolwork.

Only you can decide how important these activities are. Keep in mind that, in the case of extracurriculars, quality is more important than quantity. It's usually better to excel at one or two things—for example, to get really good at a sport or an instrument, or to become president of a club—than to superficially engage in lots of activities just so you can pad your applications.

If you're doing a menial job for a little extra spending money, can you cut your expenses so you could work fewer hours? Also ask yourself, is it really the job and extracurriculars that are causing you to study less than you should? Or is it actually a combination of other, less vital activities? According to Babcock and Marks, students appear to have reduced studying by 50 percent over the last few decades to have more leisure time, not to do more paid work or extracurriculars.[108] Something to think about.

Exercise

Think fast—how many hours a week do you spend watching TV? How about studying and doing homework? Not so easy, is it? Most of us have only a vague idea of where our time goes, so here's an awareness exercise for you to complete over one week. In the space on the following pages, write down how many hours you spend on the given activities each day. Note that you should pick a typical school week, not during finals or summer vacation.

Tip: Most top students spend more than ten hours a week studying and doing homework in high school, and more than twenty hours a week in college. If you're spending much less time than this, you might want to cut back on some nonessential activities.

Monday

Attending class: ____

Studying/Doing homework: ____

Extracurriculars/Job/Internship: ____

Commuting: ____

Exercising: ____

Chores/Family responsibilities: ___

Socializing (Dates/Parties/Hanging out): ___

Entertainment (TV/Games/Web/Movies/Shows): ___

Sleeping: ___

Other: ___

Tuesday

Attending class: ___

Studying/Doing homework: ___

Extracurriculars/Job/Internship: ___

Commuting: ___

Exercising: ___

Chores/Family responsibilities: ___

Socializing (Dates/Parties/Hanging out): ___

Entertainment (TV/Games/Web/Movies/Shows): ___

Sleeping: ___

Other: ___

Wednesday

Attending class: ____

Studying/Doing homework: ____

Extracurriculars/Job/Internship: ____

Commuting: ____

Exercising: ____

Chores/Family responsibilities: ____

Socializing (Dates/Parties/Hanging out): ____

Entertainment (TV/Games/Web/Movies/Shows): ____

Sleeping: ____

Other: ____

Thursday

Attending class: ____

Studying/Doing homework: ____

Extracurriculars/Job/Internship: ____

Commuting: ____

Exercising: ____

Chores/Family responsibilities: ____

Socializing (Dates/Parties/Hanging out): ____

Entertainment (TV/Games/Web/Movies/Shows): ____

Sleeping: ____

Other: ____

Friday

Attending class: ____

Studying/Doing homework: ____

Extracurriculars/Job/Internship: ____

Commuting: ____

Exercising: ____

Chores/Family responsibilities: ____

Socializing (Dates/Parties/Hanging out): ____

Entertainment (TV/Games/Web/Movies/Shows): ____

Sleeping: ____

Other: ____

Yes, you must include weekends, too!

Saturday

Attending class: ____

Studying/Doing homework: ____

Extracurriculars/Job/Internship: ____

Commuting: ____

Exercising: ____

Chores/Family responsibilities: ____

Socializing (Dates/Parties/Hanging out): ____

Entertainment (TV/Games/Web/Movies/Shows): ____

Sleeping: ____

Other: ____

Sunday

Attending class: ____

Studying/Doing homework: ____

Extracurriculars/Job/Internship: ____

Commuting: ____

Exercising: ____

Chores/Family responsibilities: ____

Socializing (Dates/Parties/Hanging out): ____

Entertainment (TV/Games/Web/Movies/Shows): ____

Sleeping: ____

Other: ____

CHAPTER 10

The Art of Taking Tests

You've STUDIED FOR DAYS, weeks, maybe even months for this test, and now it's finally here. You've been preparing using the smart study techniques described in the previous chapter, so you're pretty confident about the material. But you're not done yet—you need a strategy for the exam. To achieve your full test potential, you've got to keep track of your time, know what the questions are asking, and answer them in a way that will get you maximum points.

Knowing how to take a test is almost as important as studying the material. You wouldn't expect a marathoner to run a race without pacing herself, or an army to go to war without a plan of attack, or a singer to give a performance without warming up his voice, would you? Well, this is your race, your battle, your time in the spotlight, so you'd better make every moment count.

The Countdown Begins

A big part of your test performance depends on what you do the night before. Hopefully you've been spacing out your studying so you don't have to cram. You should, however, *read your review sheet* to make things fresh in your mind. Next, get your test supplies ready so you don't have to rush in the morning. Bring at least two pens (in case one runs out of ink), two pencils (in case one breaks), an eraser, a watch, your book(s) if it's an open-book test, a calculator if needed, and a sweater if the room gets cold.

Once that's done, take some time to relax and give your mind a rest. Chat with friends, watch some TV, play video games, or go for a walk. The most important thing you can do before the big day is *go to bed early!* Try to get at least seven or eight hours of sleep so your brain will be at its best.

In Their Own Words

"You should be finished studying for a test at least two nights beforehand. The night before should be just general review or last-minute questions. No new material the night before."

–Top student

The Morning of the Test

Your alarm clock goes off at 10 a.m. Your test begins at 10:15. You jump out of bed, splash some water on your face, throw on some clothes, and are out the door in five minutes flat. In case you were wondering, this is exactly what *not* to do the day of a test. You should give yourself some time to wake up and *eat a good breakfast*—nothing too sugary or heavy. Have an egg or yogurt for long-lasting energy that'll stay with you through the exam.

Go easy on the liquids, though, or you may find yourself studying the graffiti on the bathroom door instead of double-checking your answers later. Do some exercise, such as jogging or jumping jacks, to work off your nerves, but avoid strenuous activities that'll tire you out. Before you head off to face the day, pack some snacks and drinks for the test, if they're allowed.

Right Before the Test

You may have heard that last-minute studying is a big no-no, but that just isn't true. Of course you shouldn't cram or learn new material before an exam, but going over what you already know—such as your review sheet—is a great way to refresh your memory and get in the zone.

> **Chew your way to an A?** According to a 2011 study by Serge Onyper at St. Lawrence University, chewing gum for five minutes before an exam can help you get a higher grade, probably because it relieves tension and boosts blood flow to the brain.[109] (Choose the sugarless kind to avoid crashing later.) You'd better spit it out before the test starts, though. People who chew all the way through an exam do no better than those who go gum-less—the distraction of chewing seems to cancel out any benefit from this sticky treat.

How to Nullify Your Nerves

Have you experienced any of these symptoms before an exam— racing heart, sweaty palms, butterflies in the stomach, nausea, or a sense of impending doom? These are all signs of testophobia, a common but treatable problem among high school and college students. Here are nine ways to conquer your fear.

1. The number-one trick to staying calm? **Be prepared**. When you're confident about the material, it's much easier to keep your nerves at bay.
2. **Rushing is the enemy of calm.** Get to the exam at least ten minutes early and lay out your materials. Put your food on the floor if you have one of those tiny desks that feel like they were made for Santa's elves.

3. **Keep studying your review sheet** until you're told to put everything away; it'll help block out unwelcome thoughts.

4. **Don't overdo it on the caffeine.**

5. **Listen to some relaxing music.** (See the section on study music in Chapter 9 for ideas.)

6. **Tune out your classmates** if talking about the test makes you nervous.

7. **Focus on your breathing.** Take deep breaths and let each one out fully before you take another. In and out, in and out, one two, one two… there now, don't you feel better already?

8. **Think about what you're going to do after the exam.** (Hint: It should be something fun.)

9. You know that mantra we discussed back in the first chapter? Something like, "I am smart, I am prepared, I am ready for this test"? **Say it now.**

> ### Survey Says
>
> Among top students, last-minute studying was the most popular pre-test activity at 49 percent. However, 44 percent said they sit quietly and relax; 31 percent like to chat with fellow students; and 13 percent listen to music. (The total is more than 100 percent because students could choose more than one answer.)

Taking Care of Business

When you get the exam, your first impulse is probably to rip into those questions like a lion into a zebra carcass—but you should take care of a few things first. Make sure you write your name (and any other required information) at the top of your exam or on each test booklet. If you have multiple booklets, number each one so your grader won't have trouble determining the order of things. Remember: A happy grader is a generous grader!

Timing Your Test

Now that you've claimed the exam as your own, it's time to start answering questions, right? Wrong! First, *flip through the test* to get a sense of how long it is and what type of questions there are, and to make sure you have all the pages. Don't read the problems at this point—it'll take too long and you'll probably just feel overwhelmed— but you should *get a glimpse of what's ahead so you can pace yourself.* It'll often say on your exam how long to spend on each section, but if not, you might want to spend half a minute deciding how to divvy up your time.

For example, if you have twenty multiple-choice questions worth two points each, ten short answers worth four points each, and one essay question worth twenty points, spend a little less than 40 percent of your time on the multiple choice, a little less than 40 percent on the short answer, and a little less than 20 percent on the essay. (Note that I said "a little less" because you want to have some time left over to check your work.)

This is easy enough to track if you have an hour to take the test, but what if your time is less easily divisible—say, forty-five minutes? Well, you know that 10 percent of 45 is 4.5, so you can quickly calculate that 20 percent is nine minutes (4.5 x 2) and 40 percent is eighteen minutes (4.5 x 4). This means you should spend about seventeen minutes on the multiple choice (remember the "little less" part), seventeen minutes on the short answer and eight minutes on the essay, leaving you with three minutes to review your exam.

You should always bring a watch to the test, but check it sparingly. If a section is taking you longer than expected, don't panic. Just close your eyes, take a few deep breaths, and keep working speedily and steadily.

Okay, you're finally ready to start answering questions. Aren't you excited? No? Well, think of it this way: starting the test brings you one step closer to *finishing* the test.

Answering Questions Out of Order

Unless the exam is an absolute breeze, don't just start with Question 1 and work straight through to the end. When you come across a question that stumps you, *skip it*. Circle the questions you're jumping over or, if you can't mark up the test, write their numbers on a piece of scrap paper. If you can make an educated guess about a question, answer it but make a small mark next to it on the exam. In other words, you're dividing the questions into three types: the ones you know (answer), the ones you're not sure about (answer but make a small mark), and the ones you're *really* not sure about (skip and circle).

After you've gone through all the questions, make a second pass in which you answer the ones you skipped to the best of your ability. As you complete each one, put a check mark next to it or cross it out on the scrap paper. It's important to break up your test like this for four main reasons:

1. Your brain will have time to process the harder questions while you're zipping through the easy ones.
2. You may see something in the test that'll make a lightbulb go off for the ones you skipped or weren't sure about.
3. Getting the easy questions out of the way will make you feel more confident and relaxed, giving you an edge on the harder ones.
4. You don't want to get stuck on a difficult question and make yourself flustered and panicky when you've still got a lot of work to do.

Keep in mind, however, that you shouldn't jump around *too* much because you'll waste time rereading the problems. If you're prepared, you should only be skipping a small number of questions—or better yet, none at all! When you're finished with all your passes, go back through the test and make sure you haven't left anything out.

Does this sound familiar? You just finished a test with forty-four multiple-choice questions, but when you look at your bubble sheet, the last row is…43? WTF!?! Don't let this happen to you. *If you skip questions on a Scantron test, do a sanity check every few minutes and make sure you're on the right row.* And if you do reach the end of the test only to find that you're one off, tell your teacher immediately. He or she might give you some extra time or a new bubble sheet to transfer your answers onto. If you're writing your answers in a test booklet, leave some room

> **Survey Says**
>
> Most top students answer questions out of order at least some of the time. Among these students, 36 percent said they do it sometimes, 20 percent frequently, and 9 percent all the time, while 11 percent do it only if the exam is hard or tricky.

for the questions you skip. If you forget to do this or need more space, make a note in the margin that you're answering this question at the end of the booklet.

Fifty Grade-A Test-Taking Tips

No matter what your exam is on, some strategies will always apply. Multiple choice, short answer, true/false, essays, and other question types all have their own sets of rules and best practices. Here's how to milk your test for all it's worth.

Multiple-Choice Questions

1. Before you look at the choices, try to **answer the question in your own words** so you're not misled by tricky wrong answers. Then see if any of the choices matches up with your answer.
2. As you read through the answers, **cross out each one you know is wrong** (process of elimination).
3. If one of the options is "All of the above" and you know that **at least two of the choices are right**, the answer is probably—guess what?—"All of the above."

4. A choice that contains **absolute words** like "always" or "never" is rarely the right answer.

5. Make sure the choice **answers the question**. It may state something true without being the right answer.

6. **Read *all* of the choices**. Even if one seems correct, there may be a better answer farther down.

7. Is one of the choices **a term you've never even heard of before**? You may start thinking, "Well, I don't know *what* this is, so it *could* be the answer," but odds are the test-maker put it in there to trick you.

8. If you must guess, **pick the answer that is longest or most complicated, or both**. The test-maker is more likely to make up wrong answers that are on the simple side.

9. If "None of the above" or "All of the above" appears **once in a blue moon**, this could mean that it's the answer.

10. Do you have "a feeling" that an answer is right, even though you aren't sure why? If you have nothing else to go on, **follow your instinct**. There's a good chance it's on to something.

11. If you must guess, **stay away from a choice that has a typo in it**—the test-maker may not have bothered to proofread the wrong answers.

12. You may have heard that your first guess is usually right and you should avoid changing your answers as much as possible. But studies show that test-takers actually change their answers from wrong to right a little over 50 percent of the time. So if you gain some new insight into a question or realize you misread it the first time, **don't be afraid to change your mind**. However, you shouldn't keep staring at the question and second-guessing yourself until you barely know what it's asking.

13. **Multiple Choice Trick.** If you have to guess on a multiple-choice question, here's a tip that test-makers don't want you to know about: *when two or more options have recurring elements, the right*

answer is probably one of these choices. Let's say you have a question—it doesn't matter what it is—with the following choices:

a. $2x + y$

b. $3y - x$

c. $2x - y$

d. $y - 4$

Since a and c are very similar, and b and d have nothing in common with anything else, the answer is probably a or c. Also note that since three out of the four choices have a minus sign, it's more likely that the answer is c) $2x - y$.

Here's a slightly more complicated scenario. Let's say you have a question with a two-part answer. For example: The _____ beat the _____ in the race.

a. zebras…horses

b. donkeys…horses

c. mules…gorillas

d. donkeys…kangaroos

It's a good bet that the answer will be b, because two of the answers mention donkeys and two mention horses, while all the other animals are mentioned once. Only b mentions both donkeys *and* horses. Put yourself in the mind of the test-maker: he or she wants to make sure you know both parts of the question. By trying to make it trickier for you (making two or more answers sound plausible), the tester's actually throwing you some major hints!

True/False Questions

14. **Be careful of over-thinking** these yes-or-no questions. Sometimes it really is as simple as it appears.

15. Remember that **all parts must be true for the statement to be true**. If any part is false, the whole statement is false.

16. If you have to guess, statements that contain **absolute words** like "always," "never," "all," or "only" tend to be false. Statements with words like "generally," "usually," and "sometimes" tend to be true.

17. If you're out of time and have to put something down, **you should probably guess "true"**—it's harder to make up false statements. However, this is where looking at tests from earlier in the semester can come in handy, as you may find that your teacher has a thing for Fs.

18. As with multiple-choice questions, **it's okay to change an answer** as long as you've got good reason to do it.

19. **Eliminate the negative.** If a statement contains a word such as "no," "not," or "cannot," *read the sentence without the negative word and determine whether it's true or false—the answer will be the opposite*. For example, "It is not true that there are no camels in the desert." Taking out the "not," we get, "It is true that there are no camels in the desert," which is clearly false. Thus the final answer is true.

    If a sentence contains *a lot* of negatives, it's time for a slightly different strategy. Here's an example: "It is not unimportant that you do not answer this question incorrectly." (Not that anyone in their right mind would actually say this, but teachers love this convoluted stuff.) The thing to remember is that *negatives cancel themselves out*. Also keep in mind that prefixes such as *dis–*, *il–*, *im–*, *in–*, *ir–*, *non–*, and *un–* make a word negative. So "not unintelligent" really means intelligent, and "not inappropriate" equals appropriate. First let's underline all the negatives:

    It is <u>not</u> <u>un</u>important that you do <u>not</u> answer this question <u>in</u>correctly.

    Since we can cancel out the two pairs of negatives ("not" and *un–*, and "not" and *in–*), the sentence simply means, "It is important that you answer this question correctly." Now why couldn't they have said that in the first place?

Short-Answer Questions or Definitions

These questions ask you to define a term or explain something in a couple of lines.

20. **Get straight to the point.** You don't have to write in full sentences, unless your teacher tells you to.
21. If more than one definition or answer can apply, **include them all**.
22. For definitions, explain what the term is and **why it's significant**.
23. For short-answer questions, the teacher probably isn't looking for a stroke of brilliance. **It's okay to give a rote response or regurgitate what was said in class**.
24. For **matching questions**, the first thing to establish is whether all the choices must be used up (a one-to-one correspondence between the terms in both columns). It'll probably say this on the test, but if not, see if the teacher will tell you. **Start with the easy ones**, and by the end the matches for the remaining terms might be staring you in the face.

Essays

Many students have difficulty budgeting their time on essay questions. Although it's good to show off your vast stores of knowledge, you shouldn't just write whatever comes into your head. A little planning goes a long way on this one. Here's how to keep your essay under control.

25. **Answer the question!** It sounds obvious, but so many students fail to do this that it must be said. Make sure you read

the question two or three times and know exactly what it's asking. Don't go off on tangents or discuss a related topic just because you wrote a paper on it.

26. **Take it easy with the outlines.** You don't have time to construct a detailed plan. Spend no more than two or three minutes deciding on your argument, the main points you want to make, and the evidence you're going to use. Jot down just enough to remind yourself what to include.

27. **Argue, don't summarize.** Most essays require more than a rundown of the facts—you have to take a stand on something. If there's more than one right answer, choose the one you can most easily defend, whether or not you agree with it.

28. **Don't beat around the bush.** State your thesis in the very first sentence of your essay.

29. If you have room, **leave some space above each line you write** so you can insert words later without making your reader go blind.

30. **Flesh it out.** Be careful of making a lot of vague statements that don't really mean anything. Your essay should be specific and detailed, even though you don't have the books in front of you. Of course your teacher won't expect you to quote texts or cite stats from memory—he or she is not that mean—but you should be able to paraphrase key passages, list major dates, name central figures, and so on. Remember: your teacher wants to see that you've been paying attention; this is your chance to strut your stuff!

31. **Don't limit yourself to the written word**. You can draw on other sources, such as the lecture, class trips, even documentaries you saw in class. When you use evidence from beyond the book, make a quick note about where you got it. For example, "As discussed in class…," "As we saw during our trip to the Metropolitan Museum of Art…," and so on.

32. **Content matters more than style** on an essay test; it's okay if your writing isn't smooth and polished.

33. **Don't forget the basics!** Use a pen that's easy to write with, and write in script if you can do so *legibly*. Your teacher may write indecipherable comments on your papers, but that doesn't mean *you* can, too.

34. **Stay away from stuff you're not sure of,** or phrase it in a way where you can't be wrong. One of the best things about essays is that you have control over what you include. Don't know whether something happened in 1905 or 1907? Play it safe by saying "the beginning of the twentieth century."

35. If time is almost up and you're nowhere near being done, **start writing in point form**. If you wrote your outline on scrap paper, now's a good time to copy it onto the exam.

In Their Own Words

"In college, tests tend to be essay based. Teachers are looking for a complete grasp of the material, and it's important to write coherently. Don't throw all concepts that come to mind on paper. Rather, choose a narrow interpretation of the question, make that reading clear, and proceed to answer in depth with a clear thesis about the part of the subject you actually know."

—Rhodes Scholar and high school valedictorian

Tips for Open-Book Exams

36. You may think you've hit the jackpot when your teacher announces an open-book test—and sometimes you're right—but all too often it's a curse in disguise. The questions may be harder than on a regular test. Sometimes they're so complicated—especially in STEM classes—that having the

book in front of you does you little good. That's why you should **study just as hard as for a regular test**; don't let the openness lull you into a false sense of security.

37. If parts of the book—such as charts, key passages, and diagrams—would be good to refer to during an exam, make sure you mark them with Post-it notes. If it's allowed, write down key facts, formulas, and concepts in the book you'll be using.

STEM Strategies: Tips for Problem-Solving Questions

38. What's the first thing you should do when taking a STEM test? **Write down key formulas on scrap paper or at the top of the exam**. You won't have to worry about blanking out in the middle of the test, and you can refer to them whenever you want. It's like having a cheat sheet without the cheating!

39. **Think about where you've seen this question before.** It's very rare that a question will not be based on a problem you did in class or for homework. The values and phrasing might be different, but if you look closely, you'll see that it's just a variation of something you already worked on. Having trouble making sense of a word problem? Start representing terms with variables, and pretty soon it may look startlingly similar to a question you've seen before.

40. *Always* show *all* your work to get maximum partial credit. This includes the formulas you're using and steps you could easily do in your head—or on the calculator.

41. **Reread complicated questions before plunging in**, and circle or underline terms to focus on what's important.

42. If you can, **do a quick estimate before solving the problem to see if your answer makes sense.**

43. **When in doubt, draw it out.** This is especially helpful for word problems involving shapes and distance. If diagrams are already provided, mark them up.

44. If you're not sure how to solve a question that contains variables, **try plugging in numbers to make it more concrete.** You may have to use positive numbers, negative numbers, and 0 to get the whole picture. If it's a multiple-choice question, plug in the choices. The most efficient way to do this is by starting with the middle value and determining if the answer is higher or lower.

45. **Don't forget those units!** Some teachers will deduct points if you leave them out, and you'll be less likely to make careless mistakes.

46. **Checking your answers** is more important on math and science tests than any other type of exam. Nobody is exempt from careless mistakes. When you can, perform the opposite operation (multiplication instead of division, squaring instead of taking the root) on your answer to see if you get the original value.

47. If you run out of time on a problem, **explain in a few words what strategy or formula you were going to use.**

Three More Tips

48. For all tests, if a question is really confusing, **don't be afraid to ask the teacher for clarification**, either by raising your hand or going up to him or her. (If your question might give something away to the rest of the class, you'd better go up.)

49. If you make a mistake when writing or solving a problem, **cross it out instead of erasing to save precious time**—*unless*

test space is limited and you need all the room you can get. Use a mechanical pencil instead of a pen so you have the option of erasing.

50. Finally, if you're almost out of time with a lot of questions to go, focus **on the easy ones that can be done quickly**. It's better to answer a few questions correctly than a lot incorrectly.

It Ain't Over 'Til It's Over

You may see all your friends handing in their tests early, but resist the urge to go with them. You put in many hours, days, even weeks or months studying for this test— why leave early just so you can save a few minutes?

> **Survey Says**
>
> Most top students don't leave exams early: only 11 percent said they're one of the first ones to leave. While 53 percent said they leave when most people do, 36 percent take as much time as possible and are among the last to hand in their tests.

When you check your work, start with the questions you made a small mark next to (the ones you weren't too sure about). *You have the greatest chance of changing these from wrong to right.* Then review the ones you were sure about, keeping an eye out for careless mistakes. Next go over the ones you *really* weren't sure about (which you initially circled) and see if any more lightbulbs have gone off.

> **Survey Says**
>
> The vast majority of top students (71 percent) said they always review their answers. Another 20 percent said they do if they have the time.

What should you do after this first round of checks? *Keep going.* Unless you're completely certain of all your answers, you should stay until pens-down time. Taking a short break—closing your eyes for a moment, stretching your arms and legs, using the restroom— can help clear your mind and give you a fresh perspective on the test.

Dealing with PTTD (Post-Traumatic Test Disorder)

The scene following a test can resemble a war zone. Desks in disarray, the rank smell of sweat in the air, students wandering around with a glazed look in their eyes—some triumphant, others defeated. A lot of people will stick around to compare answers, but I think this is a bad idea. Some students freak out when they discover their classmates picked a instead of b, whether or not these people are any better in the subject than they are.

Instead of surrounding yourself with this post-test gossip, work off your anxiety by taking a walk or a jog; and if you must check your answers right away, have a look in the textbook. Remember that you'll get the test back soon enough, with answers you can trust. And it's critical that you *review your test when you get it back*—both the wrong and the right answers. The wrong ones to learn from your mistakes; the right ones to reinforce what you know, and because you might have made a few lucky guesses along the way. You should also make sure the exam was scored correctly. If it wasn't, check out the section in Chapter 4 on how to challenge a grade.

The Problem with Asking, "Was the Test Hard?"

In the world of academics, "hard" is a relative term. Top students tend to say a test was hard if they weren't sure about every single question. Mediocre or poor students may say the same test was easy because they're relieved they passed, or because they misunderstood the questions, or perhaps because they overestimate their own abilities. So before you ask someone what they thought of the test, keep in mind that this question means different things to different people—or better yet, don't ask it at all.

Conclusion

WHEN I TOLD PEOPLE I was writing this book, I got a lot of interesting reactions. Many adults would chuckle and say, "I wish I had this book when I was younger." Others would ask me, "So, what's the secret to being a better student?"—to which I would reply that there's no one single thing you have to do; it takes many different skills and techniques. But it's not like the way to a higher GPA is shrouded in mystery, known only to a select few. Anybody can do it! A few people looked at me in bewilderment and said, "Don't you just have to study more?" This is an unfortunate misconception held by many students, past and present. Of course you have to work hard, I would tell them, but quality is more important than quantity.

The great thing about becoming a better student is that the skills you learn now will stay with you for the rest of your life. When you read a newspaper, you'll be a pro at questioning the so-called expert opinions. If you're trying to learn a new language, you'll know how to use flash cards and lists to maximize memorization. When you're at work, you'll decorate your desk with plants and take naps in the lounge. Learning how to handle difficult teachers and classmates will make you adept at dealing with bosses and colleagues. Things like mantras, spacing, and time management come in handy no matter how old you are.

As you work to become a better student, remember that learning is far more important than the numbers on your transcript. I know it can be hard sometimes to remember what you're in school for. In some places, students go crazy over a tenth of a point—but this is an unhealthy and unsustainable way to manage your education. The real reason you're in school is to grow as a person and fulfill your potential.

Every once in a while, take a step back and think of all you've accomplished. Think of how much more you know now than you did last year or even last month. Think about how you're working to achieve your goals and not letting anything stand in your way. Take pride your work, and good things will happen. Trust me.

Good luck and have fun!

Acknowledgments

None of this would have been possible without my parents. Early on, they instilled in me a love of learning and a passion for education. They have stood by me through thick and thin, from my first day of school to the day when I tossed my cap in the air. I cannot thank them enough. I also owe a huge debt of gratitude to Rob Kovner, for believing that I could do whatever I set my mind to—and making me believe it, too!

Many heartfelt thanks to my agent, Coleen O'Shea, for guiding me through the alien world of book publishing. You took a chance on me when no one else would, and every struggling author needs someone like that in their lives. I am extremely grateful to the Sourcebooks staff, especially Peter Lynch, for believing so strongly in this project; Todd Stocke, for his continued support; and Suzanna Bainbridge, for her smart edits and for making this process smooth and easy. I am so lucky to be able to work with all of you.

About the Author

Photo by Christopher Angello

Stefanie Weisman is a woman of many interests. From history to art to computer science, she's studied (and aced) it all. Stefanie was born, raised, and still resides in Astoria, New York, across the river from Manhattan. She became valedictorian of Stuyvesant High School in 1999 and is still in awe of the brilliant minds she met there. At Columbia University, she specialized in medieval European history and graduated with the highest GPA in her class. After working for several years in corporate America, Stefanie got her MA in the History of Art and Archaeology. She was a Craig Hugh Smyth fellow at New York University's Institute of Fine Arts, where she studied ancient Greek and Roman art. Around this time, Stefanie developed an interest in technology and went back to Columbia to get a BS in computer science. While there, she decided to write a book to share her wide-ranging academic experience with other students. Stefanie's hobbies include reading ink-and-paper books, watching old films, hiking, getting lost in museums, traveling the world, memorizing Shakespeare, and eating her way through New York City. In addition to writing about education, Stefanie is working on a historical-fiction novel about the ancient Minoans.

Endnotes

Introduction

1. For those of you who aren't familiar with Stuyvesant, it's a public high school in New York City that specializes in math and science. About one in four Stuy students are admitted to Ivy League colleges. Alec Klein wrote a book about it called *A Class Apart: Prodigies, Pressure, and Passion Inside One of America's Best High Schools*, and Conan O'Brien called Stuyvesant students a "glorious, beautiful rainbow of brainiacs" in his 2006 commencement speech there.

2. In the interest of full disclosure, I received the Albert Asher Green prize for the best academic performance and highest GPA in my class at Columbia College.

3. Brian Burnsed, "Yale Once Again Tops Best Law Schools Rankings," *U.S.News Education* (March 15, 2011). Accessed December 12, 2012. http://www.usnews.com/education/best-graduate-schools/top-law-schools/articles/2011/03/15/yale-once-again-tops-best-law-schools-rankings.

4. Jennifer Moses, "The Escalating Arms Race for Top Colleges," the *Wall Street Journal* (February 5, 2011). http://online.wsj.com/article/SB10001424052748703555804576102523244987128.html.

5. "Prepared Remarks of President Barack Obama: Back to School Event," The White House website (September 8, 2009). http://www.whitehouse.gov/MediaResources/PreparedSchoolRemarks.

6. "Remarks by the President in State of Union Address," The White House website (January 25, 2011). http://www.whitehouse.gov/the-press-office/2011/01/25/remarks-president-state-union-address.

Chapter 1

7. "Applying to Harvard: Frequently Asked Questions," Harvard College Office of Admissions website. Accessed December 12, 2012. http://www.admissions.college.harvard.edu/apply/faq.html.

8. "What Yale Looks For," Yale College Undergraduate Admissions website. Accessed October 16, 2012. http://admissions.yale.edu/what-yale-looks-for.

9. Anne McGrath, ed., *U.S.News & World Report Ultimate College Guide 2011* (Naperville, IL: Sourcebooks, 2010), 95.

10. Richard Arum, Josipa Roksa, and Esther Cho, "Improving Undergraduate Learning: Findings and Policy Recommendations from the SSRC-CLA Longitudinal Project," Social Science Research Council (2011): 6.

11. Arum, Roksa, and Cho, "Improving Undergraduate Learning: Findings and Policy Recommendations from the SSRC-CLA Longitudinal Project," 8.

12. Richard Arum and Josipa Roksa, *Academically Adrift: Limited Learning on College Campuses* (Chicago: The University of Chicago Press, 2011), 72.

13. Arum and Roksa, *Academically Adrift: Limited Learning on College Campuses*, 150.

14. Arum and Roska, *Academically Adrift*, 52.

15. "Job Outlook 2012," National Association of Colleges and Employers (November 2011): 24–5.

16. Sarah Needleman, "Ivy Leaguers' Big Edge: Starting Pay," the *Wall Street Journal* (July 31, 2008). online.wsj.com/article/SB121746658635199271.html?mod=hpp_us_inside.

17. Stacy Berg Dale and Alan B. Krueger, "Estimating the Payoff to Attending a More Selective College: An Application of Selection on Observables and Unobservables," *The Quarterly Journal of Economics*, Vol. 117, No. 4 (November 2002): 1523.

18.   Philip Babcock and Mindy Marks, "Leisure College, USA: The Decline in Student Study Time," *American Enterprise Institute for Public Policy Research Education Outlook*, No. 7 (August 2010): 6.

19.   Dominique Morisano, et al., "Setting, Elaborating, and Reflecting on Personal Goals Improves Academic Performance," *Journal of Applied Psychology*, Vol. 95, No. 2 (March 2010): 255–264.

20.   F. Autin and J.-C. Croizet, "Improving Working Memory Efficiency by Reframing Metacognitive Interpretation of Task Difficulty," *Journal of Experimental Psychology: General* (March 2012): 1–9. Quote comes from press release, "Reducing Academic Pressure May Help Children Succeed," American Psychological Association (March 12, 2012). http://www.apa.org/news/press/releases/2012/03/academic-pressure.aspx.

21.   Claudia Mueller and Carol Dweck, "Praise for Intelligence Can Undermine Children's Motivation and Performance," *Journal of Personality and Social Psychology*, Vol. 75, No. 1 (1998): 33–52.

22.   Lisa S. Blackwell, Kali H. Trzesniewski, and Carol S. Dweck, "Implicit Theories of Intelligence Predict Achievement across an Adolescent Transition: A Longitudinal Study and an Intervention," *Child Development*, Vol. 78, No. 1 (January/February 2007): 246–263.

Chapter 2

23.   Susan Adams, "How to Stop Procrastinating," Forbes.com (December 16, 2010). http://www.forbes.com/2010/12/16/stop-procrastinating-efficiency-leadership-careers-organization.html. Also see J. R. Ferrari and B. L. Beck, "Affective Responses Before and After Fraudulent Excuses by Academic Procrastinators," *Education*, Vol. 118, No. 4 (1998): 529–538.

24.   Sean McCrea, et al., "Construal Level and Procrastination," *Psychological Science*, Vol. 19, No. 12 (December 2008): 1308–14.

Chapter 3

25.   "Teens and Sleep," National Sleep Foundation website. Accessed December 12, 2012. http://www.sleepfoundation.org/article/sleep-topics/teens-and-sleep.

26.   American Academy of Sleep Medicine, "High-School Seniors with Excessive Daytime Sleepiness Have an Increased Risk of Depression," *ScienceDaily* (June 11, 2010). Accessed September 24, 2012. http://www.sciencedaily.com/releases/2010/06/100609083221.htm.

27.   Howard Markel, "Lack of Sleep Takes Its Toll on Student Psyches," *The New York Times* (September 2, 2003), http://www.nytimes.com/2003/09/02/health/lack-of-sleep-takes-its-toll-on-student-psyches.html; and William Dement, M.D., "Sleepless at Stanford: What All Undergraduates Should Know About How Their Sleeping Lives Affect Their Waking Lives," Stanford University website (September 1997), http://www.stanford.edu/~dement/sleepless.html.

28.   W. E. Kelly, K. E. Kelly, and R. C. Clanton, "The Relationship between Sleep Length and Grade-Point Average among College Students," *College Student Journal*, Vol. 35, No. 1 (2001): 84–86.

29.   Eric R. Eide and Mark H. Showalter, "Sleep and Student Achievement," *Eastern Economic Journal*, Vol. 38 (2012): 512–524.

30.   Robert Stickgold and Jeffrey Ellenbogen, "Quiet! Sleeping Brain at Work," *Scientific American Mind*, Vol. 19 (August/September 2008): 24, 28.

31.   Nancy Kalish, "The Early Bird Gets the Bad Grade," *The New York Times* (January 14, 2008), accessed December 12, 2012, http://www.nytimes.com/2008/01/14/opinion/14kalish.html?_r=0; and American Academy of Sleep Medicine, "College Students Sleep Longer but Drink More and Get Lower Grades When Classes Start Later," *ScienceDaily* (June 19, 2011), accessed September 22, 2012, http://www.sciencedaily.com/releases/2011/06/110614101118.htm.

32.   June Pilcher and Amy Walters, "How Sleep Deprivation Affects Psychological Variables Related to College Students' Cognitive Performance," *Journal of American College Health*, Vol. 46, Issue 3 (November 1997): 121–126.

33.   O. Lahl, et al., "An Ultra Short Episode of Sleep Is Sufficient to Promote Declarative Memory Performance." *Journal of Sleep Research*, Vol. 17, No. 1 (March 2008): 3–10.

34.   Elizabeth Click, "A Closer Look at Napping," *NetWellness Consumer Health Information*. Accessed September 22, 2012. http://www.netwellness.org/healthtopics/sleep/napping.cfm.

35. C. Cooper, et al., "Is Caffeine Consumption a Risk Factor for Osteoporosis?" *Journal of Bone and Mineral Research*, Vol. 7, No. 4 (April 1992): 465–71; and Peggy Kraus, "Caffeine Intake Linked to Osteoporosis," Examiner.com (March 26, 2009), http://www.examiner.com/article/caffeine-intake-linked-to-osteoporosis.

36. Neil Osterweil, "Coffee and Your Health: Say It's So, Joe: The Potential Health Benefits—and Drawbacks—of Coffee," WebMD.com. Accessed September 22, 2012. http://www.webmd.com/food-recipes/features/coffee-new-health-food.

37. Francine Juhasz, PhD, "The Effects of Caffeine on Concentration," Livestrong.com (December 11, 2010), http://www.livestrong.com/article/331507-the-effects-of-caffeine-on-concentration/; and Jan Sheehan, "Does Caffeine Help Improve a Person's Memory?" Livestrong.com (June 8, 2011), http://www.livestrong.com/article/466814-does-caffeine-help-improve-a-persons-memory/.

38. Julie Edgar, "Health Benefits of Green Tea: Experts Explain Green Tea's Potential Benefits for Everything from Fighting Cancer to Helping Your Heart," WebMD.com. http://www.webmd.com/food-recipes/features/health-benefits-of-green-tea.

39. R. R. McCusker, B. A. Goldberger, and E. J. Cone, "Caffeine Content of Specialty Coffees," *Journal of Analytical Toxicology*, Vol. 27, No. 7 (2003): 520–522.

40. "Sugars and Carbohydrates," American Heart Association website. Accessed December 12, 2012. http://www.heart.org/HEARTORG/GettingHealthy/NutritionCenter/HealthyDietGoals/Sugars-and-Carbohydrates_UCM_303296_Article.jsp.

41. See, for example, R. Molteni, et al., "A High-Fat, Refined Sugar Diet Reduces Hippocampal Brain-Derived Neurotrophic Factor, Neuronal Plasticity, and Learning," *Neuroscience*, Vol. 112, No. 4 (July 19, 2002): 803–14; M. I. Sweeney, et al., "Feeding Rats Diets Enriched in Lowbush Blueberries for Six Weeks Decreases Ischemia-induced Brain Damage," *Nutritional Neuroscience*, Vol. 5, No. 6 (January 2002): 427–31; L. E. Murray-Kolb and John L. Beard, "Iron Treatment Normalizes Cognitive Functioning in Young Women," *American Journal of Clinical Nutrition*, Vol. 85, No. 3 (March 2007): 778–787; F. Darios and B. Davletov, "Omega-3

and Omega-6 Fatty Acids Stimulate Cell Membrane Expansion by Acting on Syntaxin 3," *Nature*, Vol. 440 (April 6, 2006): 813–817; and J. Ingwersen, et al., "A Low Glycaemic Index Breakfast Cereal Preferentially Prevents Children's Cognitive Performance from Declining throughout the Morning," *Appetite*, Vol. 49, No. 1 (July 2007): 240–244.

42. "Food Groups: How Much Food from the Protein Foods Group Is Needed Daily?" USDA MyPlate.gov website (June 4, 2011). http://www.choosemyplate.govfood-groups/proteinfoods_amount_table.html.

43. Fiona Macrae, "Water on the Brain: Grey Matter Literally Shrinks without Hydration," MailOnline.com (May 20, 2010), http://www.dailymail.co.uk/health/article-1279840/Water-brain-Grey-matter-literally-shrinks-hydration.html; and Matthew Kempton, et al., "Dehydration Affects Brain Structure and Function in Healthy Adolescents," *Human Brain Mapping*, Vol. 32 (2011): 71–79.

44. Margaret McCartney, "Waterlogged?" *British Medical Journal* (July 2011): 343.

45. University of Nottingham, "Boosting Brain Power—With Chocolate," *ScienceDaily* (February 22, 2007). Accessed September 22, 2012. http://www.sciencedaily.com/releases/2007/02/070221101326.htm.

46. For a rundown on some of these studies, see "Physical Activity and Student Performance at School" by Howard Taras in *Journal of School Health*, Vol. 75, No. 6 (August 2005): 214–18; and "Physical Education, School Physical Activity, School Sports and Academic Performance," by François Trudeau and Roy Shephard in *International Journal of Behavioral Nutrition and Physical Activity*, Vol. 5 (February 2008): 1–12

47. John Ratey, "The Naperville Phenomenon." Accessed September 22, 2012. http://www.johnratey.com/.

48. Charles Hillman, et al., "The Effect of Acute Treadmill Walking on Cognitive Control and Academic Achievement in Preadolescent Children," *Neuroscience*, Vol. 159, No. 3 (March 2009): 1044–1054.

Chapter 4

49. *Engage to Excel: Producing One Million Additional College Graduates with Degrees in Science, Technology, Engineering, and Mathematics,* Executive Office of the President: President's Council of Advisors on Science

and Technology (February 2012), C7. Accessed December 12, 2012. http://www.whitehouse.gov/sites/default/files/microsites/ostp /pcast-engage-to-excel-final_Februarypdf.

50. Kevin Rask, "Attrition in STEM Fields at a Liberal Arts College: The Importance of Grades and Pre-Collegiate Preferences" (a working paper), Cornell University, School of Industrial and Labor Relations site (March 2010): 6. Accessed September 23, 2012. http:// digitalcommons.ilr.cornell.edu/workingpapers/118/.

51. Donald Norman, *The Design of Everyday Things* (New York: Basic Books, 1988), 42–43.

52. *Fostering Student Engagement Campuswide—Annual Results 2011*, National Survey of Student Engagement (Bloomington, IN: Indiana University Center for Postsecondary Research, 2011), 18. Accessed December 12, 2012. http://nsse.iub.edu/NSSE_2011_Results/pdf /NSSE_2011_AnnualResults.pdf.

53. Alexander W. Astin, *What Matters in College: Four Critical Years Revisited* (San Francisco: Jossey-Bass, 1993), 236–241, 302–310, 371–372.

Chapter 5

54. Kevin Rader, "Indiana Schools Ending Cursive Writing Requirement," WTHR.com (June 29, 2011). Accessed December 12, 2012. http://www.wthr.com/story/14999729/indiana-schools -ending-cursive-writing-requirement.

55. John McLeish, *The Lecture Method* (Cambridge, UK: Cambridge Institute of Education, 1968), 10.

56. Deborah DeZure, Matthew Kaplan, and Martha Deerman, "Research on Student Notetaking: Implications for Faculty and Graduate Student Instructors," *CRLT Occasional Paper*, No. 16 (2001): 1–8. Accessed September 22, 2012. http://www.crlt.umich.edu/sites /default/files/resource_files/CRLT_no16.pdf. Also see Kenneth Kiewra, et al., "Note-Taking Functions and Techniques," *Journal of Educational Psychology*, Vol. 83, No. 2 (June 1991): 240–245.

57. J. Hartley and A. Cameron, "Some Observations on the Efficiency of Lecturing," *Educational Review*, Vol. 20, No. 1 (1967): 30–37; and M. J. Howe, "Notetaking Strategy, Review and Long-Term Retention

of Verbal Information," *Journal of Educational Research*, Vol. 63, No. 6 (1970): 285. Also see E. A. Locke, "An Empirical Study of Lecture Note Taking among College Students," *Journal of Educational Research*, Vol. 71, No. 2 (1977): 93–99.

58. Carrie Fried, "In-Class Laptop Use and Its Effects on Student Learning," *Computers & Education,* Vol. 50 (2008): 910.

59. Eyal Ophir, Clifford Nass, and Anthony Wagner, "Cognitive Control in Media Multitaskers," *Proceedings of the National Academy of Sciences*, Vol. 106, No. 37 (August/September 2009): 15583–15587.

60. Clifford Nass quoted by Adam Gorlick, "Media Multitaskers Pay Mental Price, Stanford Study Shows," Stanford University website (August 24, 2009). Accessed December 12, 2012. http://news.stanford.edu/news/2009/august24/multitask-research-study-082409.html.

61. Fried, "In-Class Laptop Use and Its Effects on Student Learning," 910.

62. Vicki Mayk, "Wilkes University Professors Examine Use of Text Messaging in the College Classroom," Wilkes University website, (November 29, 2010). Accessed on December 12, 2012. http://www.wilkes.edu/pages/194.asp?item=61477.

63. The University of Stavanger, "Better learning through handwriting," *ScienceDaily* (January 24, 2011). Accessed December 13, 2012. http://www.sciencedaily.com/releases/2011/01/110119095458.htm. Also see Anne Mangen and Jean-Luc Velay, "Digitizing Literacy: Reflections on the Haptics of Writing," *Advances in Haptics* (2010): 385-402.

64. Fried, "In-Class Laptop Use and Its Effects on Student Learning," 911.

Chapter 6

65. Trina Marmarelli and Martin Ringle, "The Reed College Kindle Study," Reed College. Accessed September 22, 2012. http://web.reed.edu/cis/about/kindle_pilot/Reed_Kindle_report.pdf.

66. Hannah Hickey, "College Students' Use of Kindle DX Points to E-Readers' Role in Academia," University of Washington website (May 2, 2011). Accessed September 22, 2012. http://www.washington.edu/news/2011/05/02/college-students-use-of-kindle-dx-points-to-e-readers-role-in-academia/.

67.   Corey Angst and Emily Malinowski, "ePublishing Working Group: Findings from eReader Project, Phase 1," University of Notre Dame website (December 21, 2010). Accessed September 22, 2012. http://www.nd.edu/~cangst/NotreDame_iPad_Report_01-06-11.pdf.

68.   Jakob Nielsen, "iPad and Kindle Reading Speeds" (July 2, 2010). Accessed September 22, 2012. http://www.useit.com/alertbox/ipad-kindle-reading.html.

69.   Jakob Nielsen, "Mobile Content Is Twice as Difficult" (February 28, 2011). Accessed September 22, 2012. http://www.useit.com/alertbox/mobile-content-comprehension.html. Also see R. I. Singh, M. Sumeeth, and J. Miller, "Evaluating the Readability of Privacy Policies in Mobile Environments," *International Journal of Mobile Human Computer Interaction*, Vol. 3, No. 1 (2011): 55–78.

70.   Alexis de Tocqueville, *Democracy in America*, Vol. 1, trans. by Henry Reeve, in Project Gutenberg (2012). Accessed December 15, 2012. http://www.gutenberg.org/files/815/815-h/815-h.htm.

Chapter 8

71.   Ben Zion Rosenfeld and Rivka Potchebutzky, "The Civilian-Military Community in the Two Phases of the Synagogue at Dura Europos: A New Approach," *Levant,* Vol. 41, No 2 (2009): 195.

72.   Steven Justice, *Writing and Rebellion: England in 1381* (Berkeley, CA: University of California Press, 1994), 9.

73.   Mortimer Chambers, Barbara Hanawalt, David Herlihy, Theodore Rabb, Isser Woloch, and Raymond Grew, *The Western Experience. Volume B: The Early Modern Era*, 7th ed. (New York: McGraw-Hill College, 1999).

Chapter 9

74.   Henry L. Roediger, III, and Jeffrey D. Karpicke, "Test-Enhanced Learning: Taking Memory Tests Improves Long-Term Retention," *Psychological Science*, Vol. 17, No. 3 (2006): 249–255.

75.   Mary A. Pyc and Katherine A. Rawson, "Why Testing Improves Memory: Mediator Effectiveness Hypothesis," *Science*, Vol. 330, No. 6002 (October 2010): 335.

76. M. K. Hartwig and J. Dunlosky, "Study Strategies of College Students: Are Self-Testing and Scheduling Related to Achievement?" *Psychonomic Bulletin & Review*, Vol. 19, No. 1 (February 2012): 126–134.

77. See, for example, R. A. Bjork and T. W. Allen, "The Spacing Effect: Consolidation or Differential Encoding?" *Journal of Verbal Learning and Verbal Behavior*, Vol. 9 (1970): 567–572; N. Kornell and R. A. Bjork, "Learning Concepts and Categories: Is Spacing the 'Enemy of Induction'?" *Psychological Science,* Vol. 19, No. 6 (June 2008): 585–592; and J. D. Karpicke and A. Bauernschmidt, "Spaced Retrieval: Absolute Spacing Enhances Learning Regardless of Relative Spacing," *Journal of Experimental Psychology: Learning, Memory, and Cognition*, Vol. 37 (2011): 1250–1257.

78. Nate Kornell, "Optimising Learning Using Flashcards: Spacing Is More Effective Than Cramming," *Applied Cognitive Psychology*, Vol. 23 (January 2009): 1297–1317.

79. Nate Kornell and Robert Bjork, "Optimising Self-Regulated Study: The Benefits—and Costs—of Dropping Flashcards," *Memory*, Vol. 16, No. 2 (2008): 125–136.

80. Colin M. MacLeod, et al., "The Production Effect: Delineation of a Phenomenon," *Journal of Experimental Psychology: Learning, Memory, and Cognition*, Vol. 36, No. 3 (2010): 671–685.

81. Steven M. Smith, Arthur Glenberg, and Robert A. Bjork, "Environmental Context and Human Memory," *Memory & Cognition*, Vol. 6, No. 4 (1978): 344.

82. Harry Grant, et al., "Context-Dependent Memory for Meaningful Material: Information for Students," *Applied Cognitive Psychology*, Vol. 12 (1998): 617-623.

83. F. F. Barbosa and F. S. Albuquerque, "Effect of the Time-of-Day of Training on Explicit Memory," *Brazilian Journal of Medical and Biological Research*, Vol. 41 (2008): 477–481.

84. J. D. Payne, et al., "Memory for Semantically Related and Unrelated Declarative Information: The Benefit of Sleep, the Cost of Wake," *PLoS ONE*, Vol. 7, No. 3 (2012): e33079. DOI: 10.1371/journal.pone.0033079.

85. Pawel Wargocki and David Wyon, "The Effects of Moderately Raised Classroom Temperatures and Classroom Ventilation Rate on the Performance of Schoolwork by Children (RP-1257)," *HVAC &*

R Research (March 2007). Accessed September 23, 2012. http://www
.thefreelibrary.com/The+effects+of+moderately+raised+classroom
+temperatures+and+classroom...-a0164997917.

86. Ruth Raanaas, et al., "Benefits of Indoor Plants on Attention Capacity
in an Office Setting," *Journal of Environmental Psychology*, Vol. 31, Issue
1 (March 2011): 99–105.

87. Atsunori Ariga and Alejandro Lleras, "Brief and Rare Mental 'Breaks'
Keep You Focused: Deactivation and Reactivation of Task Goals
Preempt Vigilance Decrements," *Cognition* (2011). DOI: 10.1016/j
.cognition.2010.12.007.

88. Kristin Nantais and E. Glenn Schellenberg, "The Mozart Effect: An
Artifact of Preference." *Psychological Science*, 10 (4) (1999), 370–373.

89. W. F. Thompson, E. G. Schellenberg, and G. Husain. (2001). "Arousal,
Mood, and the Mozart Effect." *Psychological Science*, 12 (2001), 248–251.

90. Richard Alleyne, "Playing a Musical Instrument Makes You Brainer,"
The Telegraph (October 27, 2009). http://www.telegraph.co.uk
/science/science-news/6447588/Playing-a-musical-instrument-makes-
you-brainier.html.

91. University of Calgary, "Working Alone May Be the Key to Better
Productivity, New Research Suggests," *ScienceDaily* (February 21,
2008). Accessed December 13, 2012. http://www.sciencedaily.com
/releases/2008/02/080220110323.htm.

92. Arum, Roksa, and Cho, "Improving Undergraduate Learning:
Findings and Policy Recommendations from the SSRC-CLA
Longitudinal Project," 6.

93. U.S. Department of Education, National Center for Education
Statistics, *The Condition of Education 2007* (Washington, DC: U.S.
Government Printing Office, 2007), 52.

94. Ethan Yazzie-Mintz, "Charting the Path from Engagement to
Achievement: A Report on the 2009 High School Survey of Student
Engagement," Center for Evaluation and Education Policy, Indiana
University School of Education (2010): 8. Accessed September 24,
2012. http://www.indiana.edu/~ceep/hssse/images/HSSSE_2010
_Report.pdf.

95.   Sylvia Ruiz, et al., "Findings from the 2009 Administration of the Your First College Year (YFCY): National Aggregates," Higher Education Research Institute, University of California, Los Angeles (January 2010): 8, accessed September 24, 2012, http://heri.ucla.edu /PDFs/pubs/Reports/YFCY2009Final_January.pdf; and Ray Franke et al., "Findings from the 2009 Administration of the College Senior Survey (CSS): National Aggregates," Higher Education Research Institute, University of California, Los Angeles (February 2010): 4, accessed September 24, 2012, from http://www.heri.ucla .edu/PDFs/pubs/Reports/2009_CSS_Report.pdf.

96.   Babcock and Marks, "Leisure College, USA," 1; and Arum, Roksa, and Cho, "Improving Undergraduate Learning: Findings and Policy Recommendations from the SSRC-CLA Longitudinal Project," 3.

97.   Franke et al., "Findings from the 2009 Administration of the College Senior Survey (CSS): National Aggregates," 4. Accessed September 24, 2012, from http://www.heri.ucla.edu/PDFs/pubs /Reports/2009_CSS_Report.pdf.

98.   Babcock and Marks, "Leisure College, USA," 1.

99.   Malcolm Gladwell, *Outliers: The Story of Success* (New York: Little, Brown and Company, 2008), 224–49.

100.   "Math and Science: Education in a Global Age: What the U.S. Can Learn from China," Asia Society (2006), 7.

101.   Chuansheng Chen and Harold W. Stevenson, "Motivation and Mathematics Achievement: A Comparative Study of Asian-American, Caucasian-American, and East Asian High School Students," *Child Development*, Vol. 66, No. 4 (August 1995): 1226.

102.   Bill Powell, "Five Things the U.S. Can Learn from China," *Time Magazine* (November 12, 2009). http://www.time.com/time /magazine/article/0,9171,1938734,00.html.

103.   "Education in China: Lessons for U.S. Educators," Asia Society 2005 Business Roundtable (November 2005), 6. Accessed September 23, 2012. http://asiasociety.org/files/EdinChina 2005.pdf.

104.   Craig Brandon, *The Five-Year Party: How Colleges Have Given Up Educating Your Child and What You Can Do About It* (Dallas: BenBella Books, 2010), 68–69. Also see Jeremy Rifkin, *The European Dream*

(New York: Penguin/Tarcher, 2004), 27; and Barbara Ehrenrich, *Bright-Sided: How the Relentless Promotion of Positive Thinking Has Undermined America* (New York: Metropolitan Books, 2009), 59.

105. Ralph Stinebrickner and Todd Stinebrickner, "The Causal Effect of Studying on Academic Performance," *NBER Working Paper Series*, Working Paper 13341 (2007): 20. Accessed September 23, 2012. http://www.nber.org/papers/w13341. Also see Babcock, "Leisure College, USA," 6.

106. Richard Arum and Josipa Roksa, "Are Undergraduates Actually Learning Anything?" *The Chronicle of Higher Education* (January 18, 2011), http://chronicle.com/article/Are-Undergraduates -Actually/125979/; and Arum, Roska, and Cho, "Improving Undergraduate Learning: Findings and Policy Recommendations from the SSRC-CLA Longitudinal Project," 3.

107. Victoria Rideout, Ulla Foehr, and Donald Roberts, *Generation M²: Media in the Lives of 8- to 18-Year-Olds*, Kaiser Family Foundation (January 2010), 11.

108. Babcock, "Leisure College, USA," 3–4.

Chapter 10

109. "Chewing Gum Helps Test-Takers, Research by SLU Psych Prof Shows," St. Lawrence University website (November 30, 2011). Accessed December 12, 2012. www.stlawu.edu/news/chewing gumstudy.html.

Index

Notes

Notes

14.99